The Bishop of Rwanda

JOHN RUCYAHANA

WITH JAMES RIORDAN

Published by
THOMAS NELSON™
Since 1798
www.thomasnelson.com

Published in Nashville, Tennessee by Thomas Nelson, Inc.

Thomas Nelson, Inc. titles may be purchased in bulk for educational, business, fundraising, or sales promotional use. For information, please email SpecialMarkets@ThomasNelson.com.

All Scripture quotations, unless otherwise indicated, are from The New King James Version (NKJV®), copyright 1979, 1980, 1982, Thomas Nelson, Inc., Publishers.

Page design by: Walter Petrie

Interior photo of clouds is courtesy of Walter Petrie.

Library of Congress Cataloging-in-Publication Data

Rucyahana, John.
 The bishop of Rwanda / Bishop John Rucyahana.
  p. cm.
 Includes bibliographical references.
 ISBN-13: 978-0-8499-0052-5
 ISBN-10: 0-8499-0052-2
 1. Rucyahana, John. 2. Rwanda—History—Civil War, 1994—Atrocities. 3. Genocide—Rwanda—History—20th century. 4. Reconciliation—Political aspects—Rwanda. 5. Reconciliation—Religious aspects—Church of England. 6. Bishops—Rwanda—Biography. 7. Church of England—Rwanda—Clergy—Biography. I. Title.
DT450.437.R83A3 2006
967.57104'31092—dc22
 [B]   2006024018

Printed in the United States of America

07 08 09 10 11 QW 5 4 3 2 1

I dedicate this book to my late parents, John B. Kabango and Veredian K. Karwera. Their love and encouragement never ceased and guided me even after they both died in exile. Their love remains an inspiration and a challenge to serve those in need. I also dedicate this book to the many Rwandan people who perished in terrible conditions while in exile—after being deprived of their national rights. And most of all, to all who perished in 1990–1994 during the genocide.

—John Rucyahana

This book is dedicated to my good friend, Gary Reynolds, and the men of my weekly prayer group—Wayne Kendall, Drew Horn, and David Spargur—all of whom have been there for me countless times over the years.

—James Riordan

Contents

Acknowledgments

I WAS BORN IN RWANDA IN 1945 AND BECAME A REFUGEE IN 1959 because of the first stage of the Rwandan genocide. I lived with the humiliation of statelessness and its ongoing repercussions. I am deeply in awe of the grace and kindness of God for having protected me from the time I was a youth, and as He has called me to engage and challenge some of the most difficult times in African history.

I thank God that in 1966 Jesus met me and restored my shattered hope and transformed my life for His purpose. Part of this purpose I am sharing in this book—His love, His hope, and His restoration of Rwanda.

I am so thankful for my dear wife Harriet. She has brought me great comfort and encouragement. We have lived through much together, and Harriet has encouraged me to write about all the ways we have seen God at work in our lives. Her support of me in the ministry has been, and still is, inexhaustible. Credit also goes to our five children: Grace, Patrick, Hope, Joy, and Andrew for their support and understanding. I thank God for their faith.

I give glory to God for the gift of Jim Riordan in the writing of this book. Jim is an excellent writer and his faith in Christ and life experiences made him understand the importance of reconciliation in Rwanda. Jim has been bound to my heart through the writing of this book. I hope to work with him again in writing more about Rwanda's history and plans for recovery.

My gratitude goes to Mr. and Mrs. Drayton Nabers. They continue to stand by me and support me with their honest love, counsel, prayer, and financial help. They have been used by God to bless my family. We owe them our love into eternity.

I recognize our dear Clarice McGinnis Tolbert who prays for us and makes connections for us. She fulfills the role of Philip in the Bible (John 12:20-22).

I am eternally grateful for the board members of the Mustard Seed Project for their support and love. We have shared many experiences in ministry and we have also shared our hearts.

I want to thank Rick Warren, my dear friend and brother in the Lord Jesus, for writing the foreword of this book. I pray that our efforts for reconciliation in Rwanda will bring about a healed nation.

I also want to thank Lee Hough, Beatrice Mukakalisa, and Christine Kankindi for their help. I thank those who shared their stories and all those who have chosen forgiveness and grace over hatred and revenge. My thanks also to the Prison Fellowship Rwanda staff, my diocesan staff, and all those who assist us in our efforts.

The good leadership and policies in Rwanda have made it possible for us to engage in the work of reconciliation. I acknowledge that what has been accomplished is just the beginning of this process. Please pray for Rwanda— that we, by God's grace, may persist in reconciliation, reuniting pieces scattered by the genocide. May our reconciliation teach and inspire others.

Amen.

> The Rt. Rev. John Kabango Rucyahana
> Shyira Diocese, Rwanda

I'D LIKE TO THANK THE FOLLOWING: MY DAUGHTER ELICIA, MY SON Chris, his wife Stacy, and my wife Deborah for their encouragement throughout the writing of this book; Lee Hough for bringing me into this project, and Bill Myers for suggesting me to Lee; Beatrice Mukakalisa, Joni Mohr and her husband Larry, as well as Jeff Hays for helping me assemble the information.

Also, my pastors, Jeff Crosno and Bruce Paul, for helping me through the difficult process of telling God's truth in today's world; Clark Erickson, Bev Chesterfield, Dennis Martin, Jr., Dennis and Debbie Baron, and Jeff Bass; Rich Benoit, Chris Havner, Bob Hilbrich, Murry Meents, Daryl Mest, Gary Moore, Brad O'Malley, Chad Panozzo, Doug Rapier, Gregory Samuels-El, Dave Schnell, Dan Seabolt, Andy Wheeler, Kris Whited, Jon Williamson, and the Youell family for their encouragement.

James Riordan

Foreword

Dr. Rick Warren
Author of *The Purpose Driven Life*

For several heartfelt reasons I asked for the privilege of writing the foreword for this significant book by my dear friend, Bishop John Rucyahana of Ruhengeri, Rwanda.

First, Bishop John of the Shyira diocese is one of the most extraordinary men I've ever had the privilege of knowing in traveling around the world. He is wise, compassionate, godly, energetic, thoughtful, fun, humble, and innovative. I've admired and loved this great leader from the first moment I was introduced to him by another dear friend from the Chicago area—Father William Beasley—who has been ministering with Rwandan Anglicans since 1998. Bishop John has much to teach the world about leadership in a crisis, when your life is on the line. He models servant leadership, one of the objectives of the global PEACE plan.

Second, this book is irrefutable evidence that evil really does exist in our world, that good is greater than evil, that love is greater than hate, that hope is greater than despair, and that God specializes in bringing good out of tragic circumstances. I once asked John what his purpose in ministry is today, after a million Rwandans were slaughtered in the genocide of 1994. His reply was both profound and inspiring: "We are preaching hope, standing on the bones of the past."

Third, I believe that Rwanda, if allowed to stay on its current course, will become the model of a healthy, prosperous nation, not only for all of Africa, but for every developing country in the world. In all my travels, I've never seen a country's population more determined to forgive, and to build and succeed than in Rwanda. It is miraculous that in the place with the most reason to despair, you find the most hope, the most energy, and the most cooperation. I attribute much of this to the extraordinary leadership in all three sectors of society—church, government, and business—that has risen to the task since the genocide. But there is another, even greater factor, at work in Rwanda: God is doing something special there. Jesus Christ is changing hearts and outlooks in ways that only He can. This book chronicles the spiritual renewal and reconciliation that is happening in the hearts of this country.

I have said publicly many times that it is so like God to take a small, devastated nation that the entire world turned its back on in 1994, and choose to use *that* nation to bless the rest of the world. This strong spiritual element, this "God-factor", is without a doubt the foundation of reconciliation, and the motivation underneath Rwanda's resurgence. My prayer is that it will continue to grow.

I travel to Rwanda often, because its leaders decided to be the first national model of the global PEACE plan and move toward being a purpose-driven nation. Bishop John, along with so many other Rwandan church leaders, government leaders, and business leaders, are people of purpose, committed to *"serving God's purposes in their generation"* (Acts 13:36).

The PEACE plan is an indigenous plan that uses local congregations, in cooperation with businesses and government, to tackle the five biggest problems on the planet: spiritual emptiness, a shortage of ethical servant leaders, poverty, diseases, and illiteracy/education. When Archbishop Kolini, Bishop John, President Kagame, and others first heard the plan, they each said, "We intend to be the first national model." The PEACE plan in Rwanda is a plan *by* the Rwandan and *for* Rwandans, but I have no doubt this remarkable country of wonderful people, beautiful land, and incredible opportunity will one day be helping other nations use the PEACE plan.

That's the fourth reason I'm so thrilled Bishop John has written this book. When the rest of the world realizes what the church and the people of Rwanda are becoming in the 21st century, they'll also want to know the foundation upon which it was built. I'm certain this book will be one of the classic texts that people turn to.

INTRODUCTION

Where Was God in Rwanda?

IN 1994, AT LEAST 1,117,000 INNOCENT PEOPLE WERE MASSACRED IN a horrible genocide in Rwanda, my homeland in central Africa. We are still finding bodies—buried in pits, dumped in rivers, chopped in pieces. Besides providing the details of this very sad story, my goal with this book is to tell an amazing, uplifting story. It is the story of the new Rwanda, a country that has turned to God, and which God is blessing.

It is wrong to say that Rwanda was forgotten or hated by God. That is like saying that God forgot Jesus when He was on the cross. Jesus cried out in pain because He felt forsaken, but God had not forsaken Him. God was with Him in His pain, helping Him to achieve His purpose through that pain. Rwanda was abandoned and forgotten by the world, especially by the rich and powerful nations, but God did not forget Rwanda.

Where was God when a million innocent people were being butchered?

Where was God when priests and pastors helped massacre the people in their churches?

I'll tell you where God was. He was alongside the victims lying on the cold stone floor of the cathedral. He was comforting a dying child. He was crying at the altar. But He was also saving lives. Many were saved by miracles. God does not flee when evil takes over a nation. He speaks to those who are still listening, He eases the pain of the suffering, and He saves those who can be saved. Man has free will, and God will, not override it. Sometimes evil has its day because men have so turned themselves over to it. But even then, God does not abandon them. God waits to perform a miracle.

God waited for every moment during the genocide when we would allow Him to work. For some, that happened in amazing ways right under the devil's nose, but for most of us it is happening now as God heals broken hearts and seared consciences. God has always used the broken, and He is using this broken nation to manifest His grace and power. He is taking the brokenness caused by evil and using it for a greater purpose—a great reconciliation in a nation that the world had not only given up on, but had given over to the devil, and its own evil.

I am not preaching such things from an isolated altar far away from the conflict and oblivious to the pain. I speak from Rwanda, and I speak through my own pain. My sixteen-year-old niece, whom I dearly loved, was raped and killed in a torturous, horrible way. Why would anyone go to so much trouble just to cause a young, innocent girl so much terrible pain? That is one of the questions I hope to answer in this book.

I know what it is to forgive through the tears. Like many people in Rwanda, I have to forgive in order to live. This book describes the healing of the survivors of such terrible crimes. But the pain of Rwanda is not just in the survivors of brutal acts or in those who lost someone dear to them. It is in the killers as well. It is a great burden to carry such guilt, especially when so many killed people they knew.

It does not matter that the government pushed them to do it. It does not matter that the devil reigned for a time in their hearts and minds. The guilt came and the pain stayed. That is why I have seen so many prisoners burst into tears after they have repented and been forgiven by the very people who suffered at their hands.

I've seen people forgive those who killed their loved ones. I've watched survivors and perpetrators cry together and hug each other through their tears. Something like that requires the presence of God. I could never go to a single prison to preach without the power of God. Without God, I would hate such killers with all of my heart. But with God I can truly say that I love them.

We lost more than one million people out of a population of only eight million. Of the 6.83 million who were left, 120,000 were sent to prison, but that is a fraction of those who killed. There are a great many killers who were never caught. And most of those who didn't kill helped others kill by pointing out the victims, leading the killers to the hiding places, or by watching a neighbor—perhaps their friend for years—brutally murdered along with his wife and their small children. Hacked to death with machetes. Clubbed to death by clubs with nails driven through them. Raped to death by fifty men. And worse.

The amount of pain from sorrow or guilt in Rwanda is inconceivable to those who have not been here. And the fact that so much of this pain came through the churches and other religious institutions has only made matters worse. To whom do the people turn for hope when they have been betrayed by the very ones who claim to represent God's love? During the genocide, there were pastors who killed people in their congregations; priests who bull- dozed their churches on top of the people who were hiding in them, pleading for mercy; nuns who set fire to church buildings holding people begging for their lives; and ministers who lured their congregations to their deaths with the promise of protection. Can you imagine the pain and hopelessness that generates in people?

WHEN WE TALK ABOUT RECONCILIATION IN RWANDA, WE ARE NOT just talking about reconciliation between the Hutu and Tutsi rival ethnic groups. We, the religious leadership in this country, must reconcile ourselves with the society at large. God will hold us accountable if we don't repent and change our attitudes. In the same way, the government must reconcile with the people they serve by doing their best for everyone and not playing favorites or giving in to corruption.

Ultimately, we must all be reconciled with God. In Rwanda, that means believing in God's love. It is hard for our people to see the beauty around them, because of their poverty, their pain, their suspicion, and all the abuse they suf- fered. Genocide is perhaps the most horrific human violation possible. To wipe out an entire people group and make it seem as if they never existed requires the devil's special attention.

That brings us back to the questions: *Why did God allow the massacre of more than a million people in Rwanda?* God did not want such a horrible thing, but man has free will. *Could God have stopped it?* Yes. *Why didn't He?* We cannot understand God's mind, and ultimately the only answer is that God is God and does what He wills. He is the giver of life and He is the only One who can restore life. But don't forget that there is no disaster in death for a follower of Jesus Christ—only the hope of eternal life. As Paul said in Philippians 1:21: "To live is Christ, and to die is gain" (NKJV). God is the giver of eternal life, and He can bring great good out of any situation. He raises the dead; He can also raise the broken. He can restore their hearts and minds and lift their spirits to renewed life.

In my country God is doing this today by the thousands. There is so much pain here, so many real tears, and so much guilt that our ministry is like preaching hope from the top of a pile of bones. From atop a mountain of mutilated bodies, we are stretching a hand upward to proclaim a message of transformation and recovery. And it is happening! It is my intention to show you this miracle—the miracle of God in Rwanda.

ONE

The Tragedy

IT WAS LATE. SEFA WAS THE FIRST TO HEAR THEM COMING. PETER, her husband, had long since extinguished the torches that lit their hut. But there was light flickering from under the doorway, and she could hear angry voices outside. "Peter," Sefa whispered, "are you awake? Do you hear them?"

"I hear them, Sefa. Go back to sleep. It is not our concern."

"What about what our neighbor Antoine said? Could it be the militia?"

"I told you that is rubbish, Sefa," Peter replied. "The government is not going to allow such a thing—kill every Tutsi in Rwanda. It's ridiculous!"

"But they are angry about the president."

Peter sighed. "What do we have to do with the death of the president? Such people are always angry. Go to sleep."

But then there was a loud banging on the door, and a harsh voice shouted, "Open up, you bunch of cockroaches!"

Peter instantly got out of bed and stood facing the door. "We are sleeping. Come back tomorrow."

There was a loud cracking sound, and the door to the hut shattered in pieces. Several men carrying machetes and clubs stood grinning hideously in the torchlight. One of them stepped inside. It was Ndanguza, their neighbor from up the hill. He glared at them. "But there will be no tomorrow for the cockroaches."

Sefa ran over and picked up the baby while Peter quickly pulled on his pants. Their two sons, Jacques and Edward, awoke and stared fearfully at the intruders. There were several men inside their hut now, moving toward Peter. He stood up and held out his hands as if to plead with them. "What is this, my neighbors? Do you not know me? We have lived together in this village—"

One of the men brought his machete down hard on Peter's outstretched arm, nearly hacking off his hand at the wrist. Sefa screamed, but then three men grabbed her and threw her down on the bed. They began tearing off her clothes. She saw two other men attack her boys while the others chopped at Peter as he lay bleeding on the floor of the hut. Two men held Sefa while a third raped her. She tried to hold on to the baby, but another man took him and swung him by his feet. It all became like a dream—a terrible dream. Sefa stared at her oldest son's severed foot lying on the ground; she couldn't see the rest of him. As the men changed positions and a second man was on top of her, she looked at her husband. There was blood everywhere, and he was twisted in a strange position. Then she realized his head had been chopped off. His eyes were still open, but they were vacant.

The man on top of her grunted loudly, and another took his place. She looked at him. It was Nemeye, her neighbor. Last week she had shared some milk with him, and he had given her some new straw for the floor. But Nemeye's eyes were glazed over now. He looked like a madman. Then out of the corner of her eye she saw a torch. They were setting fire to the hut. She tried to move, but they still held her fast. Then the man holding her baby yelled to the man with the torch, and to Sefa's horror, they lit the baby on fire. She screamed, and the man on top of her punched her hard in the face.

Sefa awoke hours later. Her aunt and uncle were carrying her through the bush. Her entire family had been murdered and her home burned. Hate consumed her.

I WILL TELL YOU THE REST OF SEFA'S STORY LATER. I REALIZE THAT beginning with such a harsh description may be hard for some readers, but you must understand that this particular story from the genocide is relatively mild compared to many of them.

Tribal Conflict?

Unfortunately, most of the world is misinformed about the genocide in Rwanda, dismissing it as a civil war or a tribal conflict. Nothing could be farther from the truth. The extremist political parties Paramahutu and MRND, which controlled the government of Rwanda since its independence in 1962, plotted and planned for years the genocide of the Tutsi people.

They were not responding to a crisis situation or civil unrest. There was no civil war. There were mass executions of a particular group of people, executions that were greatly assisted by a major world power and that the rest of the world chose to ignore.

Preconditions for Genocide

Sociologists tell me that all the preconditions for genocide were present in Rwanda—a small, tightly controlled land area, a disciplined and orderly population, effective propaganda and communications, a lethal ideology that fostered the necessary hatred, and a well-organized army or militia. Ironically, some of these things are good things.

Rwanda is a small country. Before the Belgians colonized us, the country was quite large, but huge sections were given to the Congo and Uganda so that Rwanda would be easier to control. And Rwanda was easier to control. That was part of the problem.

Rwanda always has had a disciplined and orderly population. In general, most of our people just want to provide for their families without any trouble from the government or anyone else. They tend to obey those in power because the last seventy-five years taught them that to question authority only leads to pain and suffering. But what about when that authority is wrong, when that authority is ordering you to commit heinous acts of violence against a great many people, some of whom you know are totally innocent?

If you were a peasant in the Rwandan countryside in 1994, you obeyed the government. You assumed they knew more than you, for they were learned men with college educations and great power.

The greatest cause of the genocide was the Hutu's hatred of the minority Tutsi people. The best way to understand such hatred usually is to examine the differences between the two groups. Alas, that is the single greatest error made by those trying to understand the Rwandan genocide. There were virtually no differences between the Tutsi and the Hutu in Rwanda that were not manufactured by forces outside of the country.

The reason for this is simple. Hutus and Tutsis lived in peace together for five hundred years. During that time they intermarried so much that the physical appearance of a modern Rwandan is a blend of both groups. Some books written about the genocide have tried to imply that one can easily tell Tutsis and Hutus apart. That would be like going to America and saying that you can easily tell an Irishman and a Norwegian apart. Like America's ethnic mix, there are few, if any, pure-blooded Hutus or Tutsis in Rwanda.

Five hundred years ago one could have found differences. The Tutsi, for example, were much taller and thinner. The Swahili word for Tutsi is *Watusi*. The average height of a pure-blooded Tutsi in the early 1900s was close to seven feet. There are old films showing Rwandan kings visiting Belgium in the thirties, wearing elaborate feathered headdresses and robes and towering over everyone.

Pure-blooded Tutsis have thinner noses than pure-blooded Hutus. Some even think that the similarity of the Tutsi nose to that of the white man is one of the reasons the Belgians chose to favor them over their Hutu counterparts when Rwanda was first colonized. Pure-blooded Tutsis are also slightly darker than Hutus, and their hair is straighter than the Hutus. But being taller, darker, having smaller noses and straighter hair is just the stereotype. Even before intermarriage with the Hutus, many Tutsis were shorter with broader noses.

My point is that you can't tell a Tutsi and a Hutu apart by physical appearances. I am a Tutsi, but when visitors ask me whether I am Tutsi or Hutu, I ask, "Which do you think I am?" They almost never get it right. I am of average height and have lighter skin and somewhat of a broad nose. Stereotyping a person is always unwise, but during the genocide many tall, dark complex-ioned men died because of their appearance.

To make such stereotyping even more ridiculous, Rwanda, like most African countries, is a patrilineal society. Our ethnicity is determined by the line of the father. A person could have pure-blood Hutu ancestry on his mother's side and a very mixed Hutu-Tutsi ancestry on his father's side, but as long as the father is considered a Tutsi, the child will be considered a Tutsi as well.

What is so ironic about the genocide in Rwanda is that people had to use government-issued identity cards to recognize the persons they were sup-posed to hate and kill. The government spent a great deal of time and money issuing identity cards in the years prior to the genocide for just that purpose. Yet amid all this propaganda-inspired hatred, very few realized that if there had been clear differences between the Hutu and the Tutsi, they would not have needed the identity cards.

The government of Rwanda performed the genocide because of a deep hatred their generation had for the Tutsis. But that hatred was not tribal based. The Hutu and Tutsi are not different tribes. Different tribes speak dif-ferent languages, live in separate areas, and have different customs. The Hutus and Tutsis of Rwanda speak the same language, have lived side by side for cen-turies, and have the same customs and traditions.

I was surprised when I visited a Chicago museum in 2003 and noticed that according to a map of Africa, Rwanda had three languages—Hutu, Tutsi, and Twa. (Twas are pygmies and make up less than 1 percent of the population.) This is how bad the tribal misconception has become. Since people think we have three tribes, they assume we have three languages. We are not different tribes, but different ethnic groups who lived together in peace for more than five hundred years.

Then the Belgians colonized Rwanda. They applied the old European method of divide and conquer, to make Rwanda easier to control. So the Belgians kept the Tutsi king and made the Tutsi chiefs taskmasters over the Hutus and the common Tutsis and had schools teach that Tutsis were supe-rior. They claimed the Tutsis were descended from Ham, Noah's son in the

Bible, and that they had ties to the ancient Egyptians and other "noble" people. The Tutsis began to believe this, and the Hutus became downcast, began to feel inferior, and their resentment began to build.

In the late fifties, the Tutsi king began to object to the way the Belgians treated the Rwandans. The Hutus and the Tutsis were forced to build roads and provide crops for the Belgians in what amounted to slave labor. The Tutsi king abolished this servitude and applied to the United Nations for independence. The Belgians had the king killed and staged what became known as the "Hutu Revolution."

There was no revolution! The Belgians took the ruling power from the Tutsis and gave it to the Hutus in the hopes that this would forestall Rwanda's push for independence. The maneuver did not work, however, and the Hutus also pushed for independence. Pressured by other colonial nations, the Belgians gave in, and Rwanda gained its independence in 1962.

But that did not undo the damage. While the Hutus and Tutsis lived together in peace in villages across the country, the Hutus who had been "educated" by the Belgians still had deep resentments for the Tutsis, whom they began to refer to as "cockroaches," and other demeaning terms. The new government denied the Tutsis many things, including decent employment and education. But that was not enough.

The government began to talk about what they called the "final solution," which meant eliminating every Tutsi man, woman, and child. The Hutu extremist government was dependent on the aid of France. They asked France to help them acquire weapons and to train their militias in more effective methods of torture and killing. The government assumed that if France helped them, neither the United Nations nor any of the superpowers would stop them from performing a national massacre. And they were right.

Now, after 1,117,000 deaths, the international community has apologized to Rwanda repeatedly. Some of these apologies are real—backed up by actions. Some of the apologies were just "good politics." God does not play politics. God has always loved Rwanda, even in its darkest hours. I believe that He is going to show that love by making an example of our country. Here is a poor African country, ripped to pieces by hatred and unfathomable cruelty, which I believe God is raising up as a shining example of what happens when a nation turns its heart to Him.

Someday soon I believe that the world will call Rwanda greatly blessed.

TWO

Setting the Time Bomb

A Brief History

The history of Rwanda not only provides clear insight into the causes of the genocide, but also gives a good perspective on the roots of the struggles we face in modern-day Africa. A few nations have benefited from colonization, but in most cases the damage far outweighs any benefit. The Germans colonized Rwanda in 1897, and were content with a loose, indirect rule. When the Belgians took over in 1916, after World War I, things remained pretty much the same until their active colonization policy was implemented in 1926.

At that time there were three ethnic groups living in Rwanda: the Hutu made up about 80 percent of the population, the Tutsi just under 20 percent, and the Twa less than 1 percent. All three groups lived in relative peace. It would be wrong to say that Rwanda was a land of peace and idyllic harmony, but there was no trace of systematic violence between the Tutsi and Hutu. There were many wars, but they pitted what was called the Banyarwanda as a group against foreign nations or tribes.

This is not to say there wasn't occasional fighting between the local chiefs, but there was no such thing as a universal Hutu-versus-Tutsi animosity. They were considered equals, they intermarried, they served in the same army, and they were in the service of the same king. It is true that the king was a Tutsi, but there were many chiefs—both Hutu and Tutsi. The king had Hutu wives as well as Tutsi wives. He had Tutsi servants as well as Hutu servants.

The question is how—after living together in virtual peace for hundreds of years—did such a murderous hatred arise, a hatred that resulted in the brutal massacre of more than a million people? And how did such hatred gain control in fewer than two generations? What happened between 1926 and 1994 that changed a somewhat primitive but peaceful society into the monsters of the genocide?

The sad truth is that this hatred was created and manipulated by the Belgian colonial masters in order to make the people easier to control. Our nation was much larger than it is today, and the Rwandan king was powerful. He had a solid administration and an economy that worked. He had power and the communication to keep it.

The first thing the Belgians did was weaken the kingdom by attaching a large piece of it to the Congo, where they had firmer control. This deprived the kingdom of many of its subjects. Then they attached another large parcel of land to Uganda, and Rwanda became even smaller. It would now be impossible for the king to regroup his people and rebel against the Belgian rule.

The Belgians still felt it necessary to have division in a country where everyone lived together and spoke the same language. If there were no natural divisions they could use, the colonial masters were not above creating them. As soon as the Belgians took power, they decided to favor the Tutsi over the Hutu and began placing the Tutsis as taskmasters over their Hutu countrymen.

There are several possible reasons for this choice. The king of Rwanda at the time of the Belgian occupation was a Tutsi, and a long line of Tutsi kings had preceded him. But while the most powerful man in the country may have been a Tutsi, there were many Hutu chiefs under him who had as much power as any of the other Tutsis, and there was no social class system dividing the Tutsis and Hutus.

The Belgians may have chosen to favor the Tutsi over the Hutu because of the Hamaic myth. First proposed by British explorer and sociologist John

Hanning Speke, the Hamaic myth is based mostly on the fact that Tutsis, with their great height and Caucasoid noses, appeared more "regal" and therefore must be descended from a prominent line of people. The Bible refers to Noah's son Ham as black, and so Tutsis were assumed to be Ham's descendants. For similar reasons Tutsis were also thought to have descended from great Egyptian Pharaohs or from the family of Solomon and the queen of Sheba. The third and most logical reason the Belgians chose to favor the Tutsis was that the Tutsis looked more like the white man.

The motivation behind the Belgians' favoritism was to divide the population of Rwanda to make them easier to control. This was used to completely draw the Tutsis in so they would feel that they were closer to white people. And it worked—some of them really came to believe they should be favored. It wasn't just the Belgians who taught these myths; they also were taught in the church schools and in the churches. The churches were not just teaching people how to be good disciples of Jesus Christ; they were teaching them how to be good servants of their colonial masters.

Using racial discrimination to control the population and separate the two major ethnic groups of the country had disastrous results. Though the differences were manufactured by the Belgians, they became real and apparent when the colonial masters began favoring Tutsis. The British used this method with great success in Uganda, but it was easier to apply there because they were dealing with two actual tribes, the Baganda and Winyuro, who tended to live separately and spoke different languages.

In Uganda the British used one king to fight another king, and eventually the enmity between these two neighboring tribes escalated. When King Kabaka Mwanga of the Winyuro rebelled against the British, he not only fought against the imperial power but against the Baganda, the neighboring tribe. They fought for seven years. The resentment between the two tribes exists to this day. When a Winyuro is angry, he will swear at or curse the Baganda.

Some historians have suggested that the animosity between the Hutus and the Tutsis was an accidental by-product of the Belgian-imposed system of order. It is more accurate to say that the tragic results of this system were not intended. There was nothing accidental about the animosity. It was created and intended as a means of controlling the Rwandan people. It was just not intended to get so out of control that it led to genocide.

Like all colonial masters, the Belgians exploited African resources. There was very little regard for Africans as human beings. The colonizing nations believed the African brain did not function like their own brains, and saw them as second-class beings, somewhere between themselves and the animals in the jungle. To dismantle their strength and remove any threat from this subhuman race was not an ethical problem for them. The Belgians were not happy with King Yuhi V Musinga, the Tutsi ruling Rwanda when they took power. During World War I, when the Germans occupied Rwanda (along with Burundi and Tanzania), they conscripted the Rwandan army to fight along-side them against the Congolese and Belgians. King Musinga's forces were great archers, and they inflicted a high number of casualties on the Belgian forces. The king was just showing loyalty to his German "friends," but the Belgians resented him for it.

Also, Bishop Classe, a powerful Roman Catholic bishop, hated Musinga because he refused to embrace Christianity. King Musinga was a very proud man and did not understand Christianity and refused to be converted by force. He continued to practice paganism. So, while he was popular with the people, King Musinga had powerful enemies and was not in a position to oppose the new standards that the Belgians began to adopt and enforce in Rwanda.

One of the first things the Belgians did was take away any power the Hutu had in the government. Before colonization many local chiefs were Hutus, so the Belgians replaced most of them with Tutsis. Each local chief always had three equal subchiefs, one of whom was nearly always a Hutu. The Belgians took away most of the power of the subchiefs to make certain that the Tutsi dominated. By the end of the Belgian occupation, 43 chiefs out of 45 were Tutsi, as well as 549 subchiefs, out of a total of 559.[1]

The Belgians considered themselves owners of all Rwanda's land. No matter how many people were living on a piece of property, the Belgians claimed the right to force them to vacate; and the Belgians then disposed of the land in any way they saw fit. This often led to Tutsi chiefs gaining control of Hutu landholdings, especially in the northwest and southwest. These and other measures caused the Hutu to decline from a status of inferiority-balanced-by-complementary into that of a quasi-rural proletariat.

By the end of the century, the vast majority of Hutu peasants owned nothing and had to continually labor just to survive. The Tutsi realized the Belgians were restructuring Rwandan society on their terms and in their favor, so they went along with it without much protest.

At this point a curious thing happened. The scientific community of the day, especially anthropologists, began to give credence to the myth of Tutsi superiority. In effect, they legitimatized the present by projecting it into the past, purporting to show that Tutsi dominance had always existed. This distorted version became the accepted theory. Identifying the Tutsi as a superior race, justified through revising history, was a better explanation for the present situation than the real complexities of history.

Acceptance of this by the Rwandan people led to an alteration of their social consciousness. Even the Tutsi peasants, who didn't benefit from the new system in any way, began to believe that they were indeed a superior race. They may have been steeped in poverty and dressed in the same rags as their Hutu neighbors, but under those rags a "finer" heart was beating.

The Hutus began to believe that they were indeed inferior. The result was that they began to hate all Tutsis, even those who were poor. If all Tutsis were superior, then all should be hated. They failed to grasp that when the Belgians were forcing the people to build roads and made the Tutsis the taskmasters—driving and beating the people to work—they were beating Tutsi workers as well as Hutu. When the Belgians brought in Congolese soldiers to beat the workers, it was both Tutsis and Hutus who were doing the work and receiving beatings.

The Belgians didn't want to be seen as the taskmasters, but their people designed the projects, their engineers planned them, and their chosen taskmasters enforced them. When they took the cows from the Rwandans to make shoes for their soldiers who were fighting the Germans in World War II, most of the cows belonged to Tutsis. But with time these truths were lost and the

Hutus' hatred was focused on their Tutsi brothers, as the Belgian colonizers intended. And after winning their freedom, when the Hutus in power looked back on their suffering, they did not see it as a time of Rwandan pain; they saw it as a time of Hutu pain.

The changes the Belgians instituted between 1926 and 1930 not only made Rwanda efficient and centralized, but also brutal. Rwanda had escaped the bulk of the slave trade because they were so far inland, but now they experienced slavery of a different kind, one that, although it allowed them to live in their native country, was no less cruel.

The increase in forced labor made life more and more miserable for the local peasantry. They were required to build and maintain roads and permanent structures, dig anti-erosion terraces, and grow coffee and other crops to export. If they did not comply, they were brutally beaten. Consequently, many Rwandans began leaving their country for Uganda, a British colony where they could be hired and paid to work.

By 1930, King Musinga's enemies had persuaded the Belgian governor that his occasional protests and heathen lifestyle were becoming a problem, and he was exiled to Kamembe and then taken farther into the Congo to the Katanga area—then called Elizabethville. He was replaced with one of his sons, Mutara III Rudahigwa. Mutara was installed as king without any of the prescribed rituals, and many people thought of him as "Mwami w'abazungu" or "King of the Whites." The Belgians loved him for a time. He often wore Western clothes, drove his own car, and was monogamous. He soon converted to Christianity. In October 1946, he consecrated the entire country of Rwanda to Christ.

It was so politically advantageous to convert to Christianity while under Belgian rule, that one has to question it. Catholic missionaries wrote about the massive conversions, and Rwanda was soon known as the "most Catholic country in the world." But were these actual conversions or more a surrender to the occupying army? What the Catholic missionaries called conversion was quite different from what we understand it to be today. Conversion then meant saying some words and going through some rituals. To be truly converted is to be convinced that you need to surrender your heart to God; it results in a new knowledge, a witness in your heart to the truth.

Mutara knew that his father had been forced into exile because of the Roman Catholic leadership, especially Bishop Classe. Knowing that the same bishop had enthroned him, conversion may have been more a surrender to the powerful for survival, rather than a matter of the heart. He was very suspicious of the Belgians and the missionaries. That's not conversion. And that's one reason many churches in Africa are not trusted. That's why they call us "colonial churches."

Mutara was extremely intelligent, but it was a natural intelligence; he had not received much classical education. He had been taught to read and write and learned French on his own; he was very sharp politically. Eventually Mutara began to encounter situations for which there were no easy choices. As the Belgians continued developing their colony, the increased demands in forced labor caused more and more dissension.

Most of the difficulty had to do with the road-building program. When the people were building roads through the mountains, they would often have to work under very risky conditions, climbing with heavy tools on their backs and working with dynamite. Often people were killed. They were scared and began refusing to work in these places. Sometimes they would run away or hide in the mountains. After all, the people were not being paid, and it was difficult for them to see the necessity of some of the roads. The Belgians forced them to work under these conditions by beating them with whips.

Seeds of Democracy

By the 1940s, Mutara had visited several European countries and began to learn about democracy and other things that awakened him to the conditions in Rwanda. He issued a decree that abolished hard labor and beatings throughout the kingdom, but the Belgians ignored it.

Mutara saw his people dedicating more and more time to the forced labor system and suffering because of it. He complained to the United Nations, and they sent a team to investigate. The team discovered Mutara's claim was true and reported everything to the UN. Belgium, France, Germany, and other nations who had colonies in Africa insisted that it was the only way to get the people to work. If these subhuman people don't understand the importance of a road, then you have to beat them to get them to build the road. And eventually they will recover from the beatings, and then they'll have the road and learn to appreciate it.

That was their reasoning.

Even if a thousand or ten thousand die to build this road, it doesn't matter. The country will get use out of it, and their descendants will also use it. It's not a great loss to lose ten thousand or even a million of these subhuman people to build the road. They have to serve the superior humans.

That was their attitude.

The Belgians thought they had Mutara under control, and then he contacted the United Nations behind their backs. This shook the Belgians' confidence in him and was the beginning of his downfall. *What is this boy doing? Where is he getting this advice?* Soon they learned that Mutara had acquired friends in Germany and America and that he was thinking about ideas like independence. They began to be suspicious of the king's every move.

As if to confirm their worst fears, Mutara began to meet regularly with other African leaders who had similar thoughts, including the highly controversial Patrice Lamumba from the Congo. In 1956, Mutara formed a political party, the UNAR, and actively started campaigning for independence. He traveled to Europe for international meetings to discuss the liberation of African nations.

Mutara realized the Belgians had deceived him when he first came into power in the 1930s and that the Belgians' heavy favoring of the Tutsis could serve as a trap. So he started to do what his fathers had done—he distributed the chiefdoms among all ethnic groups, and appointed new Hutu chiefs. This met with great disapproval from the Belgians, so Mutara took the last step, which sealed his doom. He applied for independence and campaigned throughout the country; he met with all the chiefs and asked them to resign voluntarily, so that the country could hold elections.

The Belgians realized they had let Mutara go too far. His application for independence was postponed. If they killed him outright, he would become a martyr, and his ideas would live on. So the Belgians staged what would become known as the "Hutu Revolution."

First they released Prosper Bwanakweri, a liberal Tutsi chieftain who had been imprisoned in 1954, when his liberal views began causing the king problems. Upon his release the Belgians helped Bwanakweri create the Rwandese Democratic Union (RADAR) to counter the UNAR, which was advocating for independence. By then Gregoire Kayibanda had transformed the Hutu Social Movement he had started in 1957 into what became known as the Parmehutu party. Soon there was violence between the various groups, which eventually the Belgians settled by transferring power from the Tutsi to the Hutu.

The new authorities were called *bourgmestres* after the Belgian *burgomasts;* 160 of them were Hutus as compared to 19 Tutsis. "The revolution is over," declared Belgian Colonel Guy Logiest in October 1960, and indeed it was, since the Belgians had sponsored and controlled it.[2]

On July 25, 1959, King Mutara died suddenly, most likely at the hands of the Belgians. Because Mutara left no children, the *abiru,* the court ritualists, chose his younger brother, Jean-Baptiste Ndahindurwa, to become king. Jean-Baptiste took the ritual name of Kigeli V, but although he was the next in line to the throne, he was only twenty years old and overwhelmed by the turmoil around him. He was taken prisoner by the Belgians, but soon escaped and lived in exile in east Africa, where he was incapable of providing any real leadership.

There is little question that King Mutara was moving toward a democracy and that if he had successfully established one, there would have been no reason for the "Hutu Revolution." The Belgians in all likelihood killed him and staged the revolution in the hopes of forestalling Rwandan independence. By reversing their favor the Belgians figured that the Hutus, finding themselves in power, would be satisfied with that, and the drive for Rwandan independence would subside.

Seeds of Genocide

Not only did this maneuver ultimately fail, but it also set up the genocide. Especially the Hutus active in government or wielding power inherited the shift of favor and claimed it with a vengeance. Throughout the 1950s, when I was a young boy, the racial tension began to grow. Ironically, much of it began in the churches. Church printing presses produced propaganda about how the Tutsis had been favored. Then radio talked about it, and newspapers wrote about it—and the brainwashing began!

In reality there was little financial difference between the Tutsis and Hutus during the 1950s. The up-and-down economy of the previous fifteen years did not result in the aristocratic differences, as many believed. In Gérard Prunier's fine book, *The Rwanda Crisis: History of a Genocide,* a survey conducted in the mid-1950s is quoted concerning the average incomes (excluding holders of political office) of Rwanda's three primary ethnic groups. The results were as follows:[3]

Group	# of families	Average family income (Belgian francs)
Tutsi	287	4,439
Hutu	914	4,249
Twa	2	1,446

There was virtually no difference between the Tutsi and Hutu groups. In fact, the only real discrepancy was in the Twa group, but there is such a small minority represented that not much can be gathered from that. The survey did not include the holders of political office, and this is no doubt where the most money was being made. Nonetheless, the truth is that Tutsi and Hutu peasants were at about the same financial level. It was, as in almost all Third World societies, only in the government that the discrepancy was prevalent. In one sense, the Hutu and Tutsi killed each other more because of a false perception than for any practical reason. That is what made the violence so relentless.

Practical reasons can be discussed, evaluated, and negotiated, but ideas must be pursued to their logical end, however terrible that end may be. Three hundred thousand people were killed during the "revolution," and that number did not include people who died in refugee camps from malnutrition and disease. This was a sacrifice the Belgians were willing to make to hold on to power. And, if the truth is to be told, killing an African ruler to maintain control was standard colonial procedure at that time.

The Rape of the Congo

Almost every member of King Mutara's circle of African leaders who advocated independence from their colonial masters was executed. They were crushed because the countries that colonized them didn't want to lose their resources. The Congo had great riches—rubber, minerals, oil, and diamonds. In *Leopold's Ghost,* a book about the rape of the Congo, author Adam Hochschild described his conversation with a drunken CIA man:

> That visit was in 1961. In a Leopoldville apartment, I heard a CIA man, who had too much to drink, describe with satisfaction exactly how and where the newly independent country's first prime minister, Patrice Lumumba, had been killed a few months earlier. He assumed that any American, even a visiting student like me, would share his relief at the assassination of a man the United States government considered a dangerous leftist troublemaker.[4]

The colonial rulers killed Lumumba because he talked a lot about socialist philosophies, and they were afraid he would bring the Chinese into the Congo and spread socialism. Lumumba just wanted help for his people and the only ones who would consider giving it to him were the Chinese. But these reasons are not what the people in the Congo heard. After he was dead the newspeople said that he was evil and that he was going to involve them in wars. But that was just propaganda.

It is well known that many African political leaders have been corrupt, but often their corruption is a natural progression from the international chain of corruption that ruled Africa through the colonial powers. For example, President Mabutu ruled the Congo for more than thirty years after the death of Lumumba. The World Bank and IMF gave him more loans every year. They knew that he was not using the money for the purposes for which it was publicly intended. He was depositing the money in Swiss banks. Roads and schools were not being built. Nothing was being done in the Congo.

They knew where the money was going, but they let him do it, because it kept the Congo enslaved by debt and allowed the exploitation of its minerals and other resources. They permitted Mabutu to sell out his country. Mabutu was their puppet. They let him buy villas in Paris, Brussels, and Vienna, and after he died they confiscated it all. They knew where it was, and they took it back. But the Congo remained in debt, even after they confiscated everything. Deceit and lies!

Growing Violence in Rwanda and the Tutsi Exodus

Meanwhile, the violence in Rwanda continued to grow. When Dominique Mbonyumutwa, a Parmehutu activist, was attacked and beaten by young members of UNAR on November 1, 1959, Hutu militants began attacking Tutsi chiefs and UNAR members. Many Tutsi houses were burned, and by the middle of the month, 300 people were dead and 1,231 arrested by the Belgians (919 Tutsis and 312 Hutus). In January the colonial government began to replace most of the Tutsi chiefs with Hutus, who almost immediately launched attacks on the Tutsis. This triggered another mass exodus, which eventually saw another 130,000 Tutsis leave Rwanda for neighboring countries.

The near-constant stream of Tutsi refuges between 1959 and 1964 totaled about 336,000, which broke down roughly as follows:

Burundi	200,000
Uganda	78,000
Tanzania	36,000
Zaire	22,000

Many of these were people who had joined with King Mutara after he requested all the chiefs to resign in order to begin democratic elections. After he was killed, the Belgians brought those who were leading the party with him to Ruhengeri, and they were shot in the open during daytime. They took them behind the prison on the hill that I can see from my church today. They invited the whole province to come and watch the execution.

That was another key move in dehumanizing the population. After the Tutsi began to comprehend that they could be executed, many of them began to leave. By the time elections were held in September, a great many Tutsis had left the country, and none of these people were allowed to come back in to vote. Many of the Tutsis who stayed were intimidated by the violence.

Consequently the election results showed that the Parmehutu Party received 78 percent of the vote, and the UNAR 17 percent. This meant that out of a total of forty-four seats, the Parmehutu had thirty-five and the UNAR only seven. Based on these results, Gregoire Kayibanda, founder and leader of the Parmehutu Party, became the first president of Rwanda in 1962. Despite the efforts of the Belgians, the fires of independence had been lit and refused to go out.

On July 1, 1962, under pressure from the UN, the Belgians gave in, and Rwanda was granted independence. In some ways it was a time of wonderful dreams and great possibilities. What could this new nation achieve? Where would freedom take it? But underneath this hope, a dark heart continued to beat.

THREE

The Tearing of Paradise

Rwanda During My Childhood

I was born on November 14, 1945, in Ruhengeri, Rwanda. My late father was John Baptist Kabango, and my mother's name was Verdiana. My father worked for the Belgian colonists at the local community level for twenty-seven years. I was raised near the Ugandan border, only a few miles from where our church is today.

Hutus and Tutsis Living Side by Side

When I was young, our immediate neighbors were both Hutus and Tutsis, as it was in most of the country. Just south of our house on the hill was a man named Miyira, who was a Hutu. Beside him, near the front gate of our house, was another Hutu man named Sebazungu, who was married to two wives, both of whom lived with him on the same compound. Then, directly behind us, was another Hutu man. And behind him were families of Tutsis. We were mixed—as the setting of Rwanda is to this day. To be honest, I heard little, if anything, about the differences between Hutus and Tutsis. We ate together, drank together, worked together, and played together.

The man who lived by our gate—the one with two wives—had no son; he had three young daughters. In our culture women don't eat goat meat. So whenever he wanted to eat goat meat, he would slaughter one of his goats and ask my family to send me for something, or to do something for him. And they would tell me to go over and help him, but I usually found that he had killed a goat and wanted to invite me (indirectly) to share the meal. We would feast on that goat meat together. He was a Hutu, and that's how close we were. That's how close Hutus and Tutsis were in their day-to-day relationships during that time.

During my entire boyhood, I never engaged in a single fight or even an argument with Hutus because they were Hutu. Like any children playing at school, we would sometimes fight, but not because of ethnic backgrounds. The people I remember quarreling with or fighting with were Tutsi. There was no name-calling. We simply didn't think that way.

When we were in primary school with children from different villages, we would sometimes argue or fight, but the fighting was village against village—not Hutu against Tutsi. That came later, after the propaganda in 1959, when Hutus started discriminating and shouting at Tutsis because they were told to do so.

In those days my family was a little better off than some of our neighbors, but not all Tutsis were better off than all Hutus. And at that time, if you were better off economically, you would do things to benefit your neighbors. If you had cows, you might give a cow to a neighbor. In the old days, before the king abolished servitude, people would give someone a cow and then expect service from him. But even that was done amicably and out of love. Later, people began abusing that custom and using it as a means of servitude, so the king abolished it.

But the giving of cows remained, without any element of servitude—just as a sign of love. Even rich people would exchange the gift of cows with each other, as a sign of love in the relationship. When I was young, those who were rich would employ the poor. Those who had cows would hire people to work in their herds. It was a local system to share the wealth.

Rwandans and Whites

When I was in primary school I remember I really loved Jesus, especially at Easter time when we studied the way of the Cross, and how Jesus had to suffer pain for my redemption. I really felt for Jesus then and believed that He was my friend. But later I lost a lot of that because of the way the religious leaders betrayed their faith and the people in their pews. I loved Jesus and God the Father, but didn't like those who represented Him. It was never about prejudice against the whites.

We didn't really have any white people in our community to hate except the colonists and the white clergy. It was very rare to see a white man. We knew whites were colonialists, and they were to be feared. They had to be given whatever they wanted. If they wanted cows, hens, eggs, and milk, the people would give it to them, and they would eat and leave. They were the bosses.

Even then it was the local chiefs who collected the eggs or whatever and gave them to the white person. Most of us never came in contact with a white person, and if we did, it would just be one official. So you can't really talk about discrimination. Of course, we feared the official. He might beat people or do other bad things, but he was just one person with power. That was not social discrimination as much as it was social abuse, because the colonists had no respect for Rwandans. We were considered to have less-than-human value.

Anti-Tutsi Propanda

I don't recall any problems between Tutsis and Hutus before 1959, but I know the anti-Tutsi propaganda started in 1957, and my uncle told me there were earlier incidents that began underground. The earliest one I know of involved a Roman Catholic high school in Butare, which was training the children of the chiefs. A brother there was teaching that the Tutsis persecuted the Hutus. The king of Rwanda found out about it and eventually deported him. Another priest was deported with him sometime in 1956. But it wasn't until 1957 that the newspapers began printing propaganda.

Very few people could read, so we seldom heard about any of that in the villages. And even if someone had heard about it, it would have sounded like an abomination. The printing press used for this early propaganda was in Kabwayi in the office of the archbishop of the Catholic Church. He did nothing to stop it. But it wasn't just the Catholic Church that cooperated with the

Belgians; it was all of the churches, including my church—the Anglican—at a later time. In those days, church leaders abdicated their prophetic roles and became as bad as the colonial officials. They did things concurrently; it was a joint venture to persecute the Tutsis.

President or King?

In 1959 King Mutara was killed and the Belgians wanted to make Rwanda a republic. They would still be the colonial masters, but we would elect our own leaders. The Rwandan people refused. So the Belgians crowned Kigeri, the late Mutara's brother, as king. In our culture you don't bury a king without enthroning another one. The Belgian governor wanted them to bury the king and then announce a president and pronounce Rwanda a republic. But the *abiru,* the royal ritualists, crowned a new king by force anyway. This prevented the governor from announcing a president. He realized that the people were mourning their king and they would react negatively to the announcement of a president. It could possibly have started a revolution, so he withdrew the idea.

Tutsi Homes Burned

Instead, the Belgians decided to stir up more animosity between the Tutsis and the Hutus. The governor met with Archbishop Perodin Adré, the Catholic archbishop, in Kibwayi, and they decided to try to get Hutus to burn Tutsis houses and force them to move. They wrote a letter and stamped the king's signature on it. Then they printed copies of the letter on the same printing press that was in the office of the archbishop in Kibuye. The Belgian helicopters dropped these letters with a picture of the new king on them, saying that the Tutsis had rebelled and caused the former king's death, and now the new king was appealing to the local communities to burn Tutsi homes.

The Belgians circulated this letter especially in the north and northwest, the regions that had not been politicized. It was totally false, a political manipulation to incite the local people to burn Tutsi houses, and it caused a wave of violence all over the country. Ironically, this same tactic was employed during the genocide decades later when the Tutsis were blamed for shooting down President Habyarimana's plane.

I was about fourteen, and I remember seeing Belgian helicopters flying over and dropping matches to the people on the ground so they could burn Tutsi homes. In those days, most houses were thatched grass, so they burned very easily. Then, when there was resistance, they would send soldiers in to shoot the people. If the people left, they put their belongings on lorries and moved them. They were depopulating the Tutsis from the north and moving them to the south.

The Belgians wanted to move the Tutsis from Ruhengeri, Gisenyi, and Byumba to the Nyamata area. I remember that a friend of my parents didn't want to go to Nyamata because he had grown up in the northern region, where it's colder, and he didn't want to move to the south because of malaria and geographical differences. This man's father had been a community leader, and he knew exactly what was going on.

I didn't know it at the time, but the Belgians were doing this to justify their claim that Rwanda had different tribes. This was a lie, because we don't have different tribes—both Tutsis and Hutus speak the same language, grow up in the same area, and have the same customs and culture. The Tutsi and the Hutu are different ethnic groups, not different tribes. The Belgians were trying to justify to the United Nations that there was a Tutsi zone and a Hutu zone. The separation would have only increased the animosity between the two groups, and that's part of what they wanted. But it didn't work, because most of the people stayed anyway.

Some people went into exile in the Congo; some went to Burundi, and others to Uganda. Refugee camps were set up in all the neighboring countries. In the end, about three hundred thousand people were killed and their houses burned, but they never separated into two distinct groups as the Belgians wanted.

Boarding School and the Hatred Campaign

My parents went to Uganda at this time, but they left me at the boarding school so I could finish my education. I started feeling like a refugee in my own country. I wanted to continue my education but felt as if I was hiding in the open. I was living in fear at the boarding school. There was a lot of persecution. I'd hear messages on the radio that the Tutsis were cockroaches and snakes. The radio campaign of hatred was very vigorous at that time.

After independence in 1962, the Paramahutu leaders in the government took up the Belgian campaign and made it their own. They adopted and applied it—they should have stopped it. They should have realized that as people starting a new nation, we needed to work together and promote unity and not division. They should have called the people back from exile and formed a united nation. But instead, the persecution kept growing.

I really started to hate religion during this time, because I knew that religious leaders were cooperating with the persecution. When I was about sixteen, I went to mass with my uncle, and one of the priests grabbed my belly, squeezed it hard, and said, "Your father with his sons escaped us. If it were today, we would have had him."

Here he was—a priest—squeezing the muscles of my tummy, giving me a sample of the pain that they would like to have inflicted on my family. Because we were in public, he couldn't do any more than that, but I knew that if we were in a room alone, he would have taken my head off. He had that much anger, that much hatred and bitterness—and coming from a priest! But I can still see him standing there holding my tummy to this day. I have long since forgiven him, but I wish he hadn't died. I would like to have said, "I have forgiven you." Maybe I'll meet him in heaven. If he's gone to hell—God forbid— I won't meet him there.

Move to the Congo and Intense Violence

Shortly after that they made an announcement that all Tutsi students whose parents were outside of the country were not allowed in Rwandan schools. So I had to leave Rwanda in 1962. By then my parents had left Uganda and moved to the Congo in search of land that they could farm, so I went to the Congo to join them. But in 1964 there was a move of violence in the Congo, led by a man named Murere. It became what is known now as the Mlele War. When I was nineteen, I saw what intense violence can do.

Two soldiers came into our camp and literally pulled a young woman, screaming and crying out for help, from her mother and stepfather. I was outraged that they would do such a thing. I gathered a couple of other men together, and we confronted the soldiers. They had guns, and we did not, but still we demanded that they release the young woman.

They pointed their guns at us, but we didn't back down. They cursed us, threatened us, and hit one of the men with the butt of a rifle, but we held our ground. They said they would kill us, but we just moved closer and again asked them to release her. Finally, they let her go. I think they decided that shooting us might cause more trouble than they wanted.

Uganda and My Heart's Rescue

It wasn't long after this that my parents decided to move back to Uganda. This time we went to northwest Uganda in the Bunyoro district, where we lived in a refugee camp. And it was in Bunyoro where the Lord graciously came to my rescue and saved me from my sins and desperation.

Here I was, a young man who did well in school and had expectations and ambitions for his life, and now I had been thrown out of my school and my country and was living in Uganda in a refugee camp. I was bright; I knew I could have had a career. I was very good in mathematics. I had an ambition and desire to become an engineer or a medical doctor. I knew I could have made it, but now I was a refugee.

I had thought I could have an impact on my nation, but now I lost hope and gave up expecting anything good from life. I became absorbed with the miseries of losing my university opportunities. I had lost my country and my identity; I was sinking into self-pity. I didn't really blame God for what happened, but I blamed the Belgians, and I blamed the religious leadership that had cooperated with them toward our destruction. I was very bitter.

While I was living in the refugee camp, I began going to an Anglican church, and they put out a call to teach the children in our camp. I wasn't that fond of churches, but I felt a lot of love for the poor children in the camp, so I joined with others devoted to teaching them. We didn't want them to wind up on the street or wandering in the villages, stealing food and other things. We wanted them to have a future.

It was during that time, living in a foreign land, trying to make some sense of our national origin, that I met Christ. In 1966, a year after I began teaching, He graciously accepted me in my hopelessness. I hadn't been open to God because I'd seen Rwandan religious leaders betray the truth of their religion. I'd had some Bible teaching, and during the time in the camp, I read the Bible a lot. In addition, some Christians witnessed to me. My turning point was through some of the people who talked to me one-on-one.

A lady named Mary Mukamurasa had a great influence on my life. She knew my family, and she used to tell me that I needed God in my life. We talked a lot about the difference of being in Jesus and not being in Jesus, and I realized that I needed Him in my life. When I accepted Christ, I fell to my knees in the mud and the dirt and cried to the Lord to accept my confused heart and mind.

Scripture makes it clear that God prefers to use the broken pieces. Then, whatever He does in our lives, we cannot take credit for it. Those who are proud are of little use to God. God used my hopelessness to help me surrender to Him. He had a purpose for my life through the confusion and loss of hope. But first I needed to surrender to Him. It had to be God's way. When I started reading the Bible after I accepted Jesus Christ, I began to understand.

Joseph's Dream and My Vision

In the book of Genesis, Joseph had a dream in which twelve stars and the moon bowed to him. He knew then that God was going to raise him up to a position of great authority. He didn't realize he was going to be hated, betrayed, sold, and sent to prison in order for these things to come to pass. In the same way I didn't see how God could make much out of me when I was living in the refugee camp, but after the Lord accepted me and I repented of my sins—especially my bitterness and my anger—God began to give me hope. And He gave me a vision of who I was to become.

One time as I was praying, I suddenly saw myself in clerical vestments. Another time I had a vision of my house beside the church. Then I knew that my future was not going to be determined by the Belgians or people in any government—or even by church leaders. My future was in Christ and in God the Creator.

FOUR

The Countdown

Growing Persecution

After independence in 1962, President Kayibanda realized that he couldn't get financial help from the Belgians, so he sought favor from France. France, seeing an opportunity to gain another stronghold in Africa, responded and became more and more involved in the affairs of Rwanda.

Kayibanda's government continued the persecution against the Tutsis and began to make use of the media it controlled to launch a propaganda campaign against us. In a country where more than half of the people cannot read or write and very few have televisions, radio is the dominant media. The fact that some newspapers were still printing the truth didn't matter much to the part of the population that couldn't read.

Most of the literate people were already politically aware. While an educated person might question what they read or hear from the media, the uneducated tend to accept it. The uneducated are more easily affected by threats and the emotional trauma that propaganda like this can create.

Vampire Radio

The government controlled the radio in 1994; its version of the news was what the people heard. The government station was *Radio Télévision Libre des*

Mille Collines (RTLMC), and no one else was allowed to broadcast. RTLMC was not just people shouting hate slogans all day long. While they regularly described Tutsis as "cockroaches that should be exterminated," they were smart enough to mix in popular African rock music. RTLMC employed street slang and obscene jokes to get across its racist message.

When the genocide began, some of us called it "vampire radio" because the station encouraged people to kill Tutsis. But people listened; it was hard to turn away. People were transfixed by the way the station made light of such death and destruction. It was sick and horrible, but the people who ran it knew how to make it effective. I'm told that even the RPF fighters who later came to fight against what RTLMC was advocating, listened to it rather than their own Radio Muhabura (Radio Beacon), which they found rather preachy. At least RTLMC helped the RPF become aware of just how far the Hutu radicals planned to go.

Educated to Hate

People growing up after 1962 were educated in every way against the Tutsis. It was in the media, in the schools, and even in people's conversation. Many stories were created from 1962 up to 1994 to instill hate toward the Tutsis—horrible things that Tutsis were supposed to have done to Hutus. There was no basis for most of it. When I was growing up, we very rarely encountered that kind of thing, and then it usually came from a newspaper known as *Kinyamateka*.

Many Hutus pretended to go along with the prejudicial attitudes because it tied in to their means of earning a living, either from the colonial masters or other employers. More and more you had to prove yourself loyal to the politics of the time in order to get into office. It became official in 1962, but some of it actually goes back to 1954 in some of the Catholic schools, seminaries, and teacher training colleges. People who were born in the early sixties and attended those schools were raised in it.

It wasn't like living in the villages where Hutus and Tutsis were neighbors. During the seventies the schools began reducing the number of Tutsi students, and even the few who attended were often mocked and ridiculed in the primary schools. The teachers did it almost as official policy. They would ridicule their own students—literally plan for their failure.

In some schools they would begin the morning by saying, "Tutsis, stand up!" And the Tutsi children would stand up. And then they would say, "Hutus, laugh at the Tutsis." And the Hutu children would point and laugh at the Tutsis. Children can be the most merciless executors of that kind of cruelty, especially when led by their teachers.

The government set up what they called "partitioning education," which was supposed to be structured according to the population, but they rated the Tutsis at something like 1 percent and wouldn't let them enter secondary schools, or even some primary schools. Often when it came to allowing a Tutsi to advance in school, those with the lowest scores were favored over those who performed best. It was common practice to try to weed out the brilliant Tutsi students as early as possible and promote the slower ones because they were less of a threat.

The very few Tutsi teachers who were left in the country worked under very, very difficult conditions. They were continually transferred to the worst places and were often treated badly by the administration and sometimes even by their fellow teachers. From the early sixties the Tutsi people were crushed to nothing. We had no voice. We had no strength. The government could take our property at will. We were no threat to anyone.

Changing Politics

In July of 1973, General Juvenal Habyarimana took power and ousted Gregoire Kayibanda as president. Kayibanda's regime had frustrated the elite of Rwanda, although in many ways it was idyllic. The peasants toiled away without complaining, attendance at church was at an all-time high, and the economy was good. But underneath was the growing persecution of the Tutsis and the rising hatred of the Hutu Power advocates. As the Hutu Power advocates called for stricter enforcements of the quota system for educational and employment opportunities, the Tutsis found themselves being squeezed out.

More and more of them left the country. Those who had any degree of power and wealth were eager for a change in government, and when Major

General Habyarimana took power in a bloodless coup on July 5, 1973, many Tutsis were relieved. When the new regime immediately guaranteed their security, the Tutsis believed the most severe of the persecutions were now behind them. They could not have been more wrong.

Habyarimana was unusual among African politicians at this time because he was not from a wealthy or powerful family. There were rumors that his grandfather was a poor immigrant from Uganda. He more than made up for this, however, by his marriage to Agatha Kanzinga, who came from a very highly regarded family. Agatha was from Bushiru and was the daughter of a former ruler of that province. Her Abahinza lineage amounted to a clan that the president came to rely on.

At first this group was called the "Clan de Madame" by people in the know, but later they came to be referred to as the "*akazu.*" In fact, the president's wife became so well-known as the power behind the throne that the people began to call her Kanjogers in memory of King Musinga's terrible mother, who was so powerful during his reign. While the power of her family greatly assisted Habyarimana in becoming president, it also controlled much of his administration and brought about his doom.

Habyarimana immediately pushed for increased support from France, and Paris responded. Soon France was supplying the entire government budget— from the president's salary to the salary of the people who swept the floors. It is not really accurate to say that a country is independent when all the salaries are paid by another country—especially a country that was a former colonial master in Africa. If they give you that much money, they want something in return. Basically, when the Belgians lost favor, France moved in with little difficulty. France and Belgium agreed on exploiting the nations of Africa. They had done it in the Congo and in Burundi and elsewhere.

Immediately after taking power, Habyarimana outlawed political parties. Moving toward totalitarianism, a year later he created his own political party, the *Mouvement républicain national pour la démocratie et le développement;* in English: the National Republican Movement for Democracy and Development (MRND). He publicly stated, "I know some people favor multipartyism, but as far as I am concerned, I have had no hesitation in choosing the single-party system."

Every Rwandan citizen was required to be a member of the MRND, including the children, and identity cards were issued with place of residence and ethnicity clearly marked. All *bourgmestres* and prefects were chosen from among party insiders. Every hill in Rwanda had a party cell, and just about everyone spied on everyone else in the hopes of gaining favor within the system.

People had to obtain permission to move, and unless there was a valid reason—such as going to school or getting a job—the approval to relocate was not granted. Of course, as in all party politics, a strong party connection made all the difference. It wasn't long before government control was the tightest it had ever been in Rwanda, and perhaps the tightest in the world among non-communist countries.

The Economy

By the 1970s, Rwanda's communal development labor program, initially designed to require peasants to volunteer two days of free labor out of the month for the good of the country, was often requiring four or more days. And in many cases, the work was more forced than voluntary.

Reliance on foreign aid was significant by the late 1970s and massive by the late 1980s. While representing less than 5 percent of the gross national product in 1973, foreign aid had risen to 11 percent by 1986, and to 22 percent by 1991. Much of this was because of the decline in the price of coffee, Rwanda's chief export.

In the late 1970s, coffee accounted for 75 percent of the country's exports, but prices fell steadily from 1977 to 1980, when, after a brief rise, they collapsed in 1986. Rwanda's other main export, tin, helped make up the difference in the early eighties. When it also collapsed in the mid-eighties, the economy was all but finished. Much of this was caused by the instability of the political regime, which had learned to transition from making its income primarily from coffee, tin, and tea exports to skimming off foreign aid.

By 1988 the shrinking of other revenues made the competition for foreign aid the primary activity of Rwanda's bureaucrats. Political power in Rwanda had always translated into riches, but by the late eighties it was the only game in town, and the internal struggles for power intensified accordingly.

Life in Uganda

There were many Tutsis and Hutus living together in Uganda at this time, and there were very few problems between them. There weren't even problems between the Rwandan Hutus and Tutsis who were now living together in the Ugandan camps. We ate together, and our children all attended the same schools. Hutus and Tutsis often intermarried. Few referred to each other as Hutu or Tutsi. We were even together in the churches.

After I accepted Jesus Christ into my life, God immediately encouraged me to preach the gospel. Things started to happen after I began preaching the gospel to the youth in the school where I was a teacher. After about a year of teaching, I became headmaster, and we started a program of social service in the refugee camp—thatching houses, fetching water for old women, taking children to the clinic or to school. And then I began going out to witness for Christ in the surrounding communities.

About three years after I'd accepted Christ, the bishop asked me to train as a Christian rural evangelist. So I went to the Kigezi diocese and trained under Bishop Lith, a British missionary who had organized a form of social service as acts of mercy. And we continued what I had started in the refugee camp—to go into a community and make an assessment of what they needed and then mobilize the available services.

This gave us opportunities to preach the gospel of Jesus Christ and to evangelize through social services. Show the love of Christ to them first, and then bring them to the gospel. That's how Jesus did it! I had a strong conviction that what I was doing was right, and that God wanted me to do it. I started in Bunyoro and continued for five years.

Family and Back to School!

I married Harriet on December 20, 1969. God blessed us with five children—Grace Mbabazi, born in 1970; Patrick Rukundo, born in 1972; Hope Rucyahana, born in 1975; Joy Lovinia Kabango, born in 1979; and Andrew Mpuwe, born in 1983. We also adopted, raised, and educated four orphans from my late brother's family.

In 1972 the bishop approached me about returning to school for more theological training. This was a hard thing to accept. The social services ministry I operated was becoming very effective. We had just developed an agricultural plan and were helping those who dropped out of school because of lack of finances. We were organizing loans so that they could plant three or four acres of tea; we'd help them grow it, and they paid back the loans after they harvested the crop.

I was leading people to Jesus every day in the villages. We had planted two churches in the area. I was also helping people obtain tractors to grow maize; these people, too, were becoming more open spiritually. And now the bishop was asking me to go to a theological college and sit in a classroom for three years!

I asked the bishop, "Are you really awake? Are you moving in the power of the Spirit to stop me from doing this work just to sit in a classroom? Should I abandon this work for my selfish knowledge?"

The bishop told me to pray about it, and I prayed. Then I told him, "Bishop, I have prayed, and I don't see how I can leave this work. These people are being discipled and are growing in the Lord. We'll be building a third church soon. How can I go?"

The bishop said, "John, I want to give you another point to think and pray about. God is telling me that if you don't go to train, you will reach a point where doors will be locked to you. God may want you to preach in higher circles, but if you don't train, those doors won't be opened to you." So I prayed about it. I returned and told him that if he thought it was to better the use of my life for the kingdom of God, then I would surrender to his plan.

In 1972 I began school at Bishop Tucker Theological College, Mukono

(Uganda), and I went through theological training for three years. Today, that college is called Uganda Christian University, and Steven Noll is the vice chancellor. In December 1974, I was ordained deacon and posted in Kigorobya parish, where I served for two years. In September 1975, I was ordained a priest.

In 1977 the diocese lost an influential archdeacon, Rev. Canon Kirahwa, in a car accident. Rev. Canon Kamanyire, who was the dean of the cathedral, was transferred to replace the dead archdeacon, and the bishop asked me to replace the dean of the cathedral. They also made me the senior pastor so that I did the work of the dean under the bishop. The bishop is the head of the diocese, and the archdeacons are under him; parish priests serve under them. I worked there from 1977 to 1979.

In 1980, the bishop felt that it would be good for me to continue my theological education with more advanced university training, so I went back to the college for another three years. This resulted in my obtaining a diploma in theology. So altogether I had six years of theological training, which would be equivalent to a master's degree in the United States. I graduated in 1983, and the bishop made me an archdeacon and administrator over twelve parishes and chairman of the Christian Education Committee. I held that position from 1983 to 1987.

This was during the reign of Idi Amin, during the Obote One and Obote Two regimes. I knew they were killing people in Rwanda and that Uganda was about to explode. They were singing political slogans every day, but they had no social programs, no real plan for economic recovery, nothing to really help the people. It was all propaganda without substance.

While I was at the cathedral, Idi Amin killed Archbishop Jonan Luwum. Amin lied and said it was a car accident. The truth was that when they were taking him to jail, the driver was overpowered, and Amin shot the archbishop. Then they staged the car accident. The archbishop had charged Amin with killing innocent people. I heard that Idi Amin told him, "Because you have been talking, you will talk no more" and shot him in the mouth. He had drivers run over the archbishop's body so they could say it was a car accident.

Peace at Gunpoint

Shortly after this, I had a gun pointed at my head. When Idi Amin was being overthrown and Kampala fell, they announced it over the radio. One of the people from my church went into the drum house and beat the drum. In Africa we use drums to call people to church sometimes or to announce good news to signal a time of celebration. Our area was still under Amin's control, and his soldiers thought that we were celebrating the fall of Kampala, so they arrested people in the Bible school, the pastors in the bishop's office, and came to the cathedral to arrest me.

When they came, a wave of peace washed over me. I recognized one of them and called him by name. I invited them to have tea and started talking to them without any fear. Then they asked who did the drumming last night. I said, "You gentlemen remember that the drumming started at midnight? Well, I personally went and stopped the man who was drumming—he was drunk. I then went back and about fifteen minutes later he started drumming again. Again, I went and stopped him and warned him that if he did it again, I would beat him."

They looked at their records and said, "This man is right. It was midnight. Then it stopped and started again later." They asked to see the man. They said, "If he was drunk at midnight, he must be having a hangover now." So we went to see the man. They had brought a bag of grenades and land mines. They intended to blow up the church and all the staff houses and to destroy the entire mission station. They made me sit on top of all the explosives in the truck. Imagine sitting on a bag of explosives in a truck on a bumpy road! The soldiers were foolish to do that. If the grenades had exploded, they all would have died with me in that truck.

I told the soldiers that I would take them to the man, but I wanted them to promise they wouldn't kill him. They asked why, and I said, "You can't kill him, because he was drunk. He gets drunk a lot. He didn't know that Kampala had fallen. It's just that he's a drummer—that's his work. So I'm asking you, if we find him drunk and that justifies my story, then don't kill him."

We rode to the man's house. When we found him, his eyes were red, and he smelled of crude beer. The soldiers began to beat him. I said, "Wait a minute. What about your promise?" The Lord gave me the courage to tell them to stop. But they were so angry. They were angry because they knew they were losing the war, and they were taking out their anger on us.

On the way back to the cathedral, we met another group of soldiers who were returning from taking some of our church members to jail, and when they saw us, they ran over and began to beat us. One put his gun to my head, but before he could pull the trigger, a soldier with us pushed the barrel away from my head and told him I was the one who had stopped the drumming. And then they let me go.

Several similar things happened during that time—at roadblocks and the like—but such events just strengthened our commitment to preach the gospel of the Lord Jesus Christ. During those troubles in Uganda, the churches were filled to the last space every Sunday. Many Christians were killed. Sometimes when we'd be burying one of our people, soldiers would show up and start shooting over our heads. One time everyone ran away, and I stayed and performed the burial. The soldiers were angry, but they didn't shoot me.

We would go into the street to get the bodies of our friends and church members, and soldiers would shoot at us because they wanted the bodies to lie there and rot and be eaten by the dogs in order to inflict pain on the victims' relatives. But we would take the bodies and bury them at great risk. It was the worst around the time of Idi Amin's defeat. It was physically and mentally draining, but God was using us to stand for the truth and to uphold the church. Even when there was a gun at my head, God gave me the grace not to give up, although I was afraid.

The hard thing was afterward, when you faced the day-to-day strain and there was the fear of something like that happening again. *Should I remain in this country? I'm a refugee anyway. It's not my home.* I could have run to another country. Many people fled Uganda after narrowly escaping death. *Should I run away or should I stay? Should I apply for refugee status in Canada or in America?* I was married with three children. It's a lot harder to think you might die when you have children to take care of. *Should I jeopardize my family for this church, or run away for the safety of my family?* Many times I asked God honest questions: "God, do You want me to stand and stay with the church for Your glory? What about my family and our security?"

Some of my friends told me that I was being foolish. They said, "John, you must be crazy. How do you subject your family to such danger? If you are crazy enough to risk your own life, that is one thing, but how can you risk the lives of your wife and your children? Are you sure that's God?

"Do you want to be a martyr? How can you make a difference if you die? Hasn't Africa lost enough? Do you think you are better than the other people who have run away for their lives? Are you better than Bishop Festo Kivengeri? Are you better than Mr. Sentamu who ran away from Kampala to become a priest in the UK [now the archbishop of York]?"

But it's not about that. Sentamu may have been called to run away because God had a plan and purpose in that, or a purpose for him in the United Kingdom. My younger brother, Francis Kabango, was arrested in Kampala and taken to the place of slaughter, but he was rescued by one of his students, who hid him and took him out of the country. (Today he lives in Canada.) He almost lost his life, but God graciously used one of his former students to save him.

God was calling me to stay. I could hear His voice sayin, *Don't leave this congregation. Don't leave this church.* And if God had a purpose for me to stay, even if it meant that God used my death for His glory, then I had to stay. The bottom line is that God was calling me to stay, and He delivered me through that time.

Time in America

In August 1988, the bishop sent me to Trinity Episcopal School for Ministry in Pennsylvania to get a master's degree. I majored in history and graduated in 1990. While I was in America, I realized that God had a greater purpose for bringing me there. Now I can see that every stage of development in my life, every transformation, was preparing me for the work I do now.

Following my commitment to preaching and missions, God trained me in His own way at every stage while I worked and was being educated. He was preparing me for greater challenges in my life. I believe God wanted me to interact with American society and the American church. He involved me deeply in the churches in America, not only the Episcopal, but also other denominations such as Baptist, Methodist, and independent churches. I preached in all of them.

One of the things God challenged me with was the history of American society. Because I was a history major, I studied the history of the church in America and how it interacted with society. I had the opportunity to read books about African history written from a different perspective. I saw my own experiences reflected from an American point of view, which was not involved in the colonization of Africa—an independent objective point of view about what the colonials did to Africa.

I understood many things because of this new perspective. It also gave me a deeper calling. God showed me the weakness of church leaders, not only in Africa, but also in America. What does the Episcopal Church in America—the American denomination of my church, the Anglican Church—do to reach the 105 million unchurched Americans?

What are they doing in New York? What are they doing about issues such as homosexuality and other social issues that they discuss and write book after book about? They spend millions on some things, and yet they don't seem to care about the injustices, the inner-city poor, racism, and so forth. They are the Church, and they are doing nothing!

There is some similarity to the spiritual failure in America to that in Africa. Human weaknesses are all the same. Many church leaders are building castles without a foundation, building religion without God, because Christian principles are not being applied to society. I began asking, *Why does God want me to have this knowledge? How can I apply it?*

God took me to the States not to study for my own selfish purposes, but to show me that the same weaknesses were everywhere. They were in the United Nations as an institution and in America as a rich society, just as they were in the poor African nations. Everywhere, there was a lack of commitment to what God was calling people to do. Human failure is the same everywhere. And I needed this understanding so that later I could mobilize reconciliation in Rwanda in a way that followed God's plan.

After America I went back to Bunyoro, Uganda. By that time we had a new bishop, who asked me to serve as the coordinator of Missions, Planning, and Government, which was a big office. I did that for two years and wrote new policies for the church on development and finances. But all this time I remained very active in evangelism. The same year I returned, the refugees in Uganda had a meeting and asked the president of Rwanda to let them return as full citizens of Rwanda or they would have to repatriate themselves by force. He said, "No, there is no room for you."

So they invaded in late 1990.

The Rwandese Patriotic Front

The Rwandese Patriotic Front (RPF) was a political organization dedicated to the return of exiles to Rwanda, by force if necessary. It grew out of the Rwandese Refugee Welfare Foundation that had been created in 1979 to help the victims of political oppression after the fall of Idi Amin. In 1980 the name changed to the Rwandese Alliance for National Unity (RANU), which saw itself as more militant than the previous organization.

RANU advocated the return of exiles to Rwanda, but political troubles in Uganda drove them to Nairobi from 1981 to 1986, where they led a fairly quiet existence. Much of the political turmoil centered around the disputed election of former Ugandan president Milton Obote in 1980.

In February 1981, a group of twenty-six guerrillas led by former defense minister Yoweri Musevini attacked the Kabamba Military School to secure some weapons. Two of the men involved were Fred Gisa Rwigyema and Paul Kagame. Almost five years later, when Musevini's National Resistance Army (NRA) took the capital in January 1986, three thousand of its fourteen thousand soldiers were exiles from Rwanda.

By December of the following year, finding their Rwandan nationality a hindrance to power in Uganda, Rwigyema and Kagame joined the newly named RPF. Rwigyema had never been a great advocate of returning in power to Rwanda, but for Paul Kagame, it was the only goal.

In October 1990, RPF guerrillas led by Fred Rwigyema, Peter Banyingana, and Chris Bunyenyezi invaded the Byumba province of Rwanda from Uganda. When the Rwandan government troops began to falter, French and Zairean troops were called in, and the RPF was hit with heavy losses. Among the casualties were its leaders—Banyingana, Bunyenyezi, and Rwigyema. Paul Kagame, who was in America at the time of the invasion, hurried back to take control.

The RPF appeared to be almost finished, and Kagame asked President Museveni of Uganda to let them cross back into Uganda and regroup what was left of his forces. With Museveni's help, Kagame and the balance of the RPF forces stayed in the cold mountains of the Virunga volcanoes for about two months. Wearing only light clothing at a height of five thousand meters, several soldiers froze to death, but Major Kagame was able to reorganize.

Foreshadowing of the Genocide

It is worth noting that upon hearing of the RPF invasion in Byumba, President Habyarimana and his cabinet staged a fake attack on Kigali, the capital. Gunshots rang out in the city around 1:00 a.m. and lasted until around 7:00 a.m. Although thousands of shots were fired, there was not a single casualty and very little damage to buildings. But Habyarimana and his advisors achieved their goals—the international press was deceived, and the French ambassador Georges Martre reported "heavy fighting in the capital" to his superiors in Paris. Within a few days, French troops were increased.

It is important to learn from this incident that the Habyarimana regime had no qualms about creating a false event to manipulate others to help them obtain their goals. This tendency for the dramatic was repeated with horrendous results in 1994.

Another foreshadowing of the genocide occurred in the Mutara region, where some of the defeated RPF had taken refuge. Between October 11 and 13, approximately 350 Tutsi civilians were massacred, and more than 500 homes were burned. In nearly every case the murders were planned and led by the local government authorities. Although none of the victims was a RPF fighter or a civilian supporter, the government claimed they were all RPF. When questioned about these events at a press conference, President Habyarimana replied, "Civilians? Why should we kill civilians if they are not involved in the fighting? There is no revolt. Everybody is obeying."

The government's fears resulted in a frantic recruitment drive for the RGF, the Rwandese Government Forces, in French called *Forces Armees Rwandaises* or FAR. The RGF numbered about fifty-two hundred in October 1990, grew to fifteen thousand by mid-1991, thirty thousand by the end of that year, and fifty thousand by the time the Arusha peace negotiations began in mid-1992.

Such huge growth created many problems, but weapons was not one of them—France provided all that was needed by either shipping them directly or through foreign contracts with Egypt or South Africa. The lack of consistent pay was a problem, however, as was the fact that the quality of the troops had gone down. For every man who joined because of his ideals, there were many others who did so only to eat, drink, and loot.

France's Attitude

It is also of benefit to examine France's commitment to Rwanda at this time. Why would the French send soldiers to a faraway African country to protect a faltering dictatorship from an invasion by its own refugee population trying to return home by force? The question begins quietly here, but the demand for an answer continues in an escalating pattern that ultimately leads to France's complicity in the killing of a million Tutsis.

There is no easy answer, especially considering France's tendency to intervene in the affairs of other nations whenever they have the opportunity. More than any other former colonial power in Africa, France has used military force to ensure its involvement in the affairs of its former colonies. Part of this is economics. While the riches of Africa's resources may no longer be theirs for the taking, the continent can still greatly benefit its former colonial masters by serving as an immeasurably vast money-laundering machine.

By supplying aid and seeing that overpriced government contracts are given to friends in high places, millions of dollars can be effectively manipulated for a variety of purposes. Political allies are rewarded. Indeed, entire French political parties are partially financed through this method. And during the Habyarimana years, the cooperating African government officials always got their share.

There is also the tendency for France to see the world as divided between the beloved Francophone, or French-speaking nations, and the dreaded Anglophone, or English-speaking nations. In the United Nations, French-speaking African nations vote along the same lines as France and are duly rewarded by France with commitment to aid and military help. France may have lost the battle for worldwide influence to the English-speaking nations, but they do not give up an inch of power without pushing things to the limit.

Consequently the invasion of Rwanda (Francophone) in October 1990, by an army of exiles coming from Uganda (Anglophone), was a classic example of the Anglo-Saxons' attempts to take more ground. France's perception was that French forces were being sent in to protect an ally from a foreign invasion. In the mind of Paris, the returning refugee aspect was just a cover-up. The message to the rest of Francophone Africa had to be clear—the French would not allow this kind of thing.

Unfortunately, one of the ways this message transferred to the Akuzu, the influential men close to the president, was that no matter what the government of Rwanda did, France would support it on the international stage. And they were right.

Most of the world sees the political struggle in Rwanda before the genocide as between the Hutu-extremist-dominated government and the increasingly oppressed Tutsis. But to be accurate, one has to factor in the RPF and France. On one hand you have the Habyarimana regime trying to hold on to power while the RPF's inroads were beginning to create the possibility of forced negotiations. Meanwhile the Tutsis who remained in Rwanda were playing what meager political cards they had left in the hope of ending their persecution.

The French planned to maintain their interests in Rwanda by keeping the current administration in power. Having tested his army against the RPF forces and lost, Habyarimana knew that France was his stopgap. His wife's Hutu extremist clan said he could use the power of the French to end his internal struggles as well. And now a new and terrible solution began to emerge. People were quietly whispering in the president's ear about "a final solution." And he was beginning to listen.

Mission Accomplished

Paul Kagame had two things in mind when he took his men into the Virunga Mountains. The first was to buy time to regroup, and this he clearly accomplished. In early 1991, the RPF numbered only about five thousand men, but by the end of 1992 it numbered twelve thousand, and by the time of the genocide in April of 1994, it had grown to more than twenty-five thousand.

Composed primarily of Tutsis, the RPF also included a great number of Hutus. Originally, the expatriate quality of the RPF cause led to a high standard of education for most of its troops. Almost all of them had attended primary school, about half had gone to high school, and nearly 20 percent had been to college, making the RPF probably the most well-educated guerrilla force in history. But by 1992, these high standards were declining, as very young Tutsi boys, at times almost children, joined from inside Rwanda. For those boys it was more a matter of self-defense and refuge because the persecution of Tutsis was becoming so severe.

Most of the RPF's finances came from exiled Tutsis scattered across Africa, but the RPF was never well funded. The movement's leaders led Spartan lives and were careful spenders. This was significant because African guerrilla organizations usually floundered because their leaders spent too much of the money on themselves. There was never any such financial misappropriation in the RPF, and consequently they lasted a long time.

Kagame had a second reason for choosing the Virunga Mountains as a base of operations. He was now in a position to swoop down on Ruhengeri. Attacking the northernmost province of Rwanda gave the RPF several advantages. Its mountainous location made it one of the few places they could attack long enough in advance without being detected.

Ruhengeri was also the former home of President Habyarimana. Attacking it would strike a chord of insecurity throughout the entire country and greatly add to the mythic power of the guerrilla forces. On an even more practical level, Ruhengeri contained Rwanda's largest prison, with more than a thousand prisoners, many held for political reasons.

Kagame attacked Ruhengeri on January 23, 1991, accomplishing virtually all of his objectives. When the panicked prison officials called the government offices in the capital, they were told to kill all the inmates to keep the political prisoners from joining Kagame's army. But Colonel Charles Uwihoreye, an officer at the prison, refused to carry out the executions, and the prisoners were freed when the RPF stormed the gates. Many of the newly freed men did in fact join the RPF. After holding Ruhengeri for a day, the RPF withdrew before the government forces could arrive.

In addition to freeing the prisoners, the RPF recovered a large amount of military equipment. Most importantly, however, Kagame achieved the psychological motives for the attack, and its message sent shock waves throughout Rwanda. The RPF had to be taken seriously. By March 29, 1991, a formal cease-fire was signed until negotiations could be completed. Kagame had accomplished the first part of his mission.

Persecution Grows Worse

The persecution increased after the RPF attack. Three hundred to a thousand Tutsis were killed in Kanama, Rwerere, and Gisenyi between the invasion and June of 1991. In the Bugesera region approximately three hundred

Tutsis were killed during March 1992. They rounded up people, stacked piles of wood on them, and dropped them in a pit. The district authorities with their police and their armed units carried out the executions with the help of the local people.

Before this, the government just targeted Tutsis who were educated or rich and those with influence. They would pick and kill, pick and kill. There were many smaller massacres—ten here, twenty there, and we found out later that many of those killings were for training purposes. They were training people to kill and wanted to test their methods. The numbers began to increase.

They were motivating the general population to kill as well. From the presidential office to the local leaders, everyone was encouraged to kill. The government was secretly organizing it, and the killings spread throughout different provinces. I think a lot of this was also testing for reactions. They wanted to see what the international community was going to do about it. Pretty soon they realized that the rest of the world wasn't going to do anything to prevent them from killing.

If there had been an outcry from the UN or some powerful nations, the genocide in 1994 might never have happened. But there was nothing. Also, the people of Rwanda had become conditioned to the violence. It was being accepted as a part of life.

Antoine Mupenzi, a Kinigi villager who later fled the country, remembered:

> For those of us who were left in my village in 1992, it was like we were used to the killing. The persecutions for us really began in 1990. When the RPF entered the country, the government started arresting any Tutsi they thought might be sympathetic to the RPF. My father was one of the men they picked. They put him in prison. After that we lived at home, afraid. The government was harassing us. Then, in late 1991 they started killing people near where I lived in Kinigi. Many of our friends and relatives died, and many others ran away to the Congo. It was our own neighbors that were doing the killing because of all the propaganda telling them that Tutsis were bad people and the enemy of the Hutu. They were even teaching them how to kill.[1]

Kayitsinga Faustin, a Tutsi who was in high school during this time, told about some of the persecutions he faced:

In 1990 they killed my uncle. Around that same time they started beating me at school. The Hutu students would just start beating us Tutsis every now and then. It was very hard to go to school then, but I finished school. Then when I was working, sometimes there were beatings from the other employees. One time some people came looking to beat me, and I hid with a former teacher called Rugal. He hid me from them in his house for three days. For a long time the government of Rwanda would not allow a Tutsi to join the army or appoint a Tutsi to any government office, even a very minor one. There were still a few Tutsis who had not been made to resign from the government. I was told that at one political meeting, one of the ministers told the president that he simply could not sit in a meeting with a Tutsi. He replied, "From now on, every time I come to a meeting and he is there, I will beat him. I will strike him twice every time I come into a meeting."[2]

And he stood up and struck the man in the presence of the president. Shortly after that, the one who struck the Tutsi resigned from the party. That's how bad it was for a Tutsi to be involved in anything important. Those Tutsis who dared to take up offices ended up dying for them. A man would be exposed by accepting a public office, and once everyone knew, the extremists would hunt him down and kill him. So eventually, Tutsis just accepted that they were not supposed to hold office.

The Tutsis in Rwanda began to develop the mind-set that they didn't deserve anything—that they had to stay in the background if they wanted to survive. Even the few who managed to filtrate through to the universities were always under intense fear. Though many terrible things had already happened, many people sensed that the worst was yet to come.

Journalists who wrote about the occasional massacres or discrimination against the Tutsis were fired, and sometimes even killed. Any Hutus who protested the killings or tried to help the victims were killed or jailed.

Propaganda: The Illiterate Community

By now the anti-Tutsi propaganda machine was in full force. In addition to the government radio station (RTLMC), there were wild stories and cartoons printed in the newspapers. Some were just ridiculous—cartoons showing Tutsis as having tails and big ears. Much of it was about demonizing them. There was a constant stream in the papers—story after story implying that Tutsis were bad people to the very core of their beings. After a while, this type of continual barrage can cause people who should know better to start to wonder, and by the time the word reaches the illiterate community, it's not even questioned anymore. It's just accepted as truth.

The illiterate community would hear government officials saying these things on the radio and then see that it was backed up by a news story someone told them about or a cartoon they saw. And pretty soon the younger ones, who had never known the Tutsis as their friends before all the propaganda, began to believe it. And even though people knew the "Tutsi problem" was exaggerated, such as in a cartoon, they still began to feel that there must be some truth to it. That's how this kind of propaganda works.

The Hutu Ten Commandments

One piece of propaganda that was widely circulated became somewhat of a creed for the Hutu extremists. Known as the Hutu Ten Commandments, it could be found hanging in the finest homes and public places. The heartless prejudice of the document speaks for itself. *Bahutu* refers to the Hutu ethnic group as a whole, while *Mahutu* refers to a single Hutu. *Bahutukazi* refers to Hutu women as a group.

The Ten Commandments of the Bahutu

1. Hutus must know that the Tutsi wife, wherever she may be, is serving the Tutsi ethnic group. In consequence, any Hutu who does the following is a traitor.

    • Acquires a Tutsi wife

- Acquires a Tutsi mistress
- Acquires a Tutsi secretary or dependent

2. All Hutus must know that our Bahutukazi daughters are more worthy and more conscientious in their role of woman, spouse, and mother. Are they not more beautiful, good secretaries, and more sincere?

3. Bahutukazi, be vigilant and bid your husbands, brothers, and sons to come to their senses.

4. All Hutus must know that all Tutsis are dishonest in business. Their only goal is ethnic superiority. Rizabara Uwariraye (someone who has experience in something explains it better). In consequence any Hutu who does the following is a traitor.
   - Makes alliance with the Batutsi in business
   - Invests his money or state money in a Matutsi's company
   - Lends money or borrows it from a Matutsi
   - Grants favors to the Batutsi in business (granting of import license, bank loans, busiling parcels, public tender offers . . .)

5. The strategic political, administrative, economical, military, and security positions must be reserved for the Bahutu.

6. In education, students in primary, secondary, and universities, including teachers, Hutus must be majorities.

7. The Rwandan Armed Forces must be exclusively Hutu. The war experience in 1990 teaches us this lesson. No military man should marry a Tutsi woman.

8. The Bahutu must stop taking pity on the Tutsi.

9. The Bahutu, wherever they are, must be united, interdependent, and worried about their Bahutu brother's fate. The Bahutu from the inside and outside of Rwanda must constantly look for friends and allies for

The Holy Cause begun by their Bantu brothers. They must constantly oppose the Tutsi propaganda. The Bahutu must be strong and vigilant against their common Tutsi enemy.

10. The Social Revolution in 1959, the 1961 referendum, and the Hutu ideology must be taught to all Bahutu and at all levels. All Mahutu must widely spread this message. Every Mahutu who persecutes his Mahutu brother is a traitor, for his brother has read, spread, and taught this ideology.

Rewarded for Killing

As the random massacres became more frequent, another disturbing trend developed. Those Hutu who participated were rewarded, and those who killed the most were promoted to higher positions in the army or within the police department. It became ingrained in the people that persecuting Tutsis was a good way to get ahead in life. The government sponsored and encouraged such killings even in public and on the radio, but when confronted, they would deny any killings had occurred. Sometimes they'd say the missing people must have left to join their RPF brothers outside of the country or, if bodies were found, that the RPF had killed them.

By 1993, roadblocks were set up to stop people from leaving the country. By then the government was not killing Tutsis in the hope that the rest of the Tutsis would leave the country. No, by then, they wanted to kill them all! They wanted the Tutsis to stay so that when the genocide began in full force, they could make certain they were all killed. Sometimes the government people even told the Tutsis that they should stay because things were going to get better for them.

FIVE

A Carefully Laid Plan

IN ALL LIKELIHOOD, SERIOUS PLANNING FOR THE GENOCIDE BEGAN in late 1992. In the beginning it was the extremists of course, but as time wore on, others began to take the "final solution" more seriously. More and more the extremist Hutus in the government were worrying about having to share power with the Tutsis. The RPF was just outside the capital and there was no acceptable compromise with them. The idea of solving the problem by simply murdering every Tutsi in Rwanda—and their Hutu sympathizers—began to look feasible.

By November 1992, Leon Mugesera, vice president of the Gisenyi MRND Section and an influential man within the MRND party, was openly proclaiming the idea to party militants of the Kabaya *sous-prefecture.*

> Why are we waiting to get rid of these families? . . . We have to take responsibility into our own hands and wipe out these hoodlums . . . The fatal mistake we made in 1959 was to let them [the Tutsi] get out . . . They belong in Ethiopia and we are going to find them a shortcut to get there by throwing them into the Nyabarongo River [which flows northward]. I must insist on this point. We have to act. Wipe them all out! [1]

Jean Kambanda, a cabinet member, revealed in Linda Melvern's book *Conspiracy to Murder: The Rwandan Genocide,* that the genocide was openly discussed in President Habyarimana's cabinet meetings. Kambanda described, according to Melvern, how one cabinet minister said she was personally in favor of getting rid of all Tutsis. "Without the Tutsi, she told ministers, all of Rwanda's problems would be over." [2]

Cooperation Through Fear

The planners of the genocide knew that the only way they could hope to succeed was to secure the cooperation of the Hutu peasants who so outnumbered the Tutsis in the villages across Rwanda. But the peasants had lived in peace with their Tutsi neighbors for most of their lives, and the only way they would turn on them was if they felt they had to kill to protect themselves. This fear was easiest to create by playing off the peasants' natural fear of the invading RPF army and expanding it through manipulation of the media into something that was truly terrifying.

Along with this, a plan had to be enacted to persuade government people at the local levels to encourage the killings to a point where they would appear as if it was a matter of duty for the nation. The plan hinged on the peasants living in a state of fear brought on by previous years of conflict and political confusion.

Fear played a key role in every step of the genocide. The very idea of exterminating an entire nationality of people was born out of fear in the first place. No matter who the Belgians had favored or what injustice might have been done, it was thirty-five years in the past, and by 1994, the Tutsis had already been reduced to a marginal existence. They were not allowed in schools, the army, or government services. The only jobs available to them were as drivers or servants.

People in the government were not allowed to marry Tutsi women, and those who had Tutsi women were required to make them second wives or mistresses. The Tutsi as a population were beaten down. Many people who don't know the truth think that the Tutsi were arrogant and that the Hutus reacted to that, but that is ridiculous.

How can you be arrogant when you are someone's driver or houseboy?

How can you be arrogant when you have not gone to school and you don't have the right to open a shop on the main street of any given town? Killing the Tutsis was an act of cowardice. Why kill someone you have already crushed? It's demonic. There is no better answer than that.

Weapons and Training for Killing

By March of 1992, the plotting of the genocide had extended to involve France, for it was then that the French arranged for the acquisition of machetes from China. That the weapons were actually shipped from Egypt with no mention of France underscores the secrecy of the project. The credit was extended through France's nationalized bank, Credit Lyonnais. Some reports indicate the amount was $6 million, but others claim it was only $750,000. In any case, enough new machetes were ordered so that every Hutu male in Rwanda over twelve years of age could have one.

French military experts were already training people in how to use these and other weapons. The training was done at the local levels and resulted in many Tutsis losing their lives. Many of those in prison have admitted that they were trained to kill as early as 1990, and there is ample testimony that the French were involved in teaching torture and killing techniques to members of a covert group known as the Interahamwe ("those who work together"), a group of young men who had attached themselves to the youth wing of the ruling MRND party.

It is not known if the French were involved in the kidnappings and murders of thousands of Tutsi peasants as part of these training exercises, but it is without question that it is their methods that were being tried on these unfortunate souls in the years immediately preceding the genocide. A man imprisoned for crimes during the genocide described one of these training raids to me.

It was in February of 1990. I operated a small bar at the time, and there were some Tutsis there drinking beer one night, when a Hutu man came in and said that the RPF was invading the country and we should kill all the Tutsis. I asked him why kill our neighbors when they are our friends? He just looked at me, but then a few weeks later some Hutus I knew came and got me. They had a pickup truck with eighteen Tutsis being held. They told me to get in the back and guard them. They took them somewhere where they were held for several days.

All I know is that each night they killed some of them until finally there were only three of them left. I went with them to pick up the three and one of them had been seriously beaten, but Nyirakamanzi, the local leader, told us not to bother taking him to the hospital, but just to dump him at his house. He died a little while later. I complained that we should've taken the man to the hospital, and the next thing I knew, the assistant mayor had a meeting and told me that I was being fined 25,000 francs for being sympathetic to the Tutsis. He said that if I continued doing that I would be killed. So after that, I stopped arguing for the Tutsis.[3]

At the same time these exercises were going on, other limits were being tested as well. In various parts of the country, the Interahamwe engaged in killing sprees on an occasional basis. The same prisoner told about one such event: "In March of 1990, I saw some Hutus take seven Tutsis and throw them into a small lake called the Nyirakigugu. The bottom is very muddy, and when you throw someone in, their feet get stuck in the mud and they drown. Another time I went with some Hutus and we burned a Tutsi family alive inside their house."[4]

Sometimes more than a hundred people were killed during these outbreaks. Some of this was anger and hate spilling over, and some was a calculated exercise to measure the cooperation of the local populace and the reaction of the nation as a whole. In virtually every case, the locals did as they were told, and the nation accepted the killings as a way of life. The reaction of the international community was also being gauged at this time.

In late December 1992 and early January 1993, an outbreak of violence led to a dozen people killed and more than a hundred fleeing the area. When an international commission arrived on January 7 to monitor human rights abuses, the violence stopped. The local *bourgmestres* in the area announced to the community that the violence would be reduced during the commission's visit, but that it would begin again as soon as the commission left.

In reaction to this, RPF soldiers committed one of their few acts of reactionary violence. After they took the town of Ruhengeri on February 8, 1993, they killed eight civil servants and a few of their relatives. At least one of the dead, *bourgmestre* Thaddee Gasana of Kinigi commune, had been guilty of ordering the killing of some Tutsis a few days before.

Over time, the Habyarimana regime realized that they were indeed in a position to eliminate more than a million Tutsis. The peasants would do as they were told, and no one within the country had the power to stop them. With the involvement of the French and their power at the UN, they were confident that the international community would not intervene. The stage was set.

Buying Time

The problem was the RPF. Since beginning their latest assault in February of 1993, General Kagame's forces had pushed to the outskirts of the capital before the French were again sent in to stop them. Now the UN wanted to negotiate a cease-fire, and President Habyarimana found himself in a quagmire. The only sure way to stop the RPF was to allow the negotiations, but this meant agreeing to the UN's plan for peace that involved establishing a coalition Paramahutu/RPF government and allowing the refugees to return.

The coalition was something his cabinet, and especially Madame Habyarimana's clan, the *akazu,* would never agree to. They would not divide Rwanda and share control of it with the Tutsis. Indeed, that was the purpose of "the final solution," but the RPF had to be kept at bay before the genocide could begin. There was no easy solution, but there was a way to buy time. Habyarimana gave every indication he'd sign the Arusha Peace Accords as they were drawn up, and this satisfied the RPF for the moment.

Habyarimana—Man in Power

After delaying as much as possible, he signed the agreement on August 4, 1993, but it is highly doubtful he had any intention of enforcing it. That he thought he could pull off such a delicate dance was indicative of Habyarimana's overconfidence in his ability. He was no doubt clouded by the hubris of a man in power. He was an attractive and compelling man, who looked the part of the president of an up-and-coming African nation, and he had totally won the hearts of the Hutu population. After a time, however, many began to realize that he was just manipulating them for his own advantage.

By the middle of his reign, other Hutus began to oppose him. Some of them were killed for it. The president was a great one for telling people that peace was needed while he was killing people at the same time. By the time he signed the Arusha Accords, Habyarimana was being squeezed between the *akazu,* France and the rest of the international community, and neighboring African leaders who wanted an immediate peace in Rwanda. And he had the RPF breathing down his neck. The truth is he was doomed, but he was too arrogant to realize it.

First and foremost, Habyarimana had to keep the people closest to him happy. The *akazu* were not only powerful in their own rights, but they also knew his darkest secrets. They knew the opponents he had eliminated and those he'd unjustly thrown in jail. He needed their cover, so he kept them close even when he knew they were embezzling or killing people. Their relationship was locked in by mutual damnation. Still, there were limits.

Habyarimana had tested those limits in 1989, when he wanted to allow his daughter to marry a Tutsi. She became pregnant by her boyfriend, because she knew that was the only way she might be able to stay with him, since he was Tutsi. President Habyarimana was going to allow them to get married, but the people around him protested, saying, "Our president can't let his daughter marry Amatutsi, because that will go against our ten commandments and hurt our campaign."

So the president refused to let her marry the boy and made her marry a Hutu instead, but many in the cabinet never forgave him for considering the Tutsi marriage. And signing the Arusha Peace Accords angered them further. Most of the people around the president were far more extreme in their political attitudes than he was. They were pushing for the genocide, and although he may have wanted it, Habyarimana knew the political risk he'd be taking.

A few months later, an unforeseen event tightened the noose around Habyarimana's neck. On October 21, 1993, the president of Burundi, Melchior Ndadaye, was kidnapped and assassinated by extremist Tutsi army officers. To Habyarimana, the death of a moderate like President Ndadaye was a warning about how vulnerable someone in his position could be. Compared to Habyarimana, President Ndadaye had been an idealist. As a former general, Habyarimana knew that power was better enforced through guns than pieces of paper.

If he turned the tables on the *akazu* and made a deal with the RPF or the UN, his country would be divided, and those who protected his back would turn against him in the process. If they conspired against him, he could be prosecuted for the killings or questioned about his use of public money. There was no clear path, and his only avenue was to find ways to delay the process until a solution could be found.

For those advocating the genocide, however, the assassination of a beloved Hutu president by traitorous Tutsis played right into their hands. The psychological impact of this on the Rwandan Hutu population was driven home by the arrival of hundreds of thousands of Hutu refugees from Burundi who quickly spread tales of massacres at the hands of the Tutsi army of Burundi. Another important piece in the genocide puzzle had fallen into place. Later, the Hutus who had fled into Rwanda from Burundi would become very active in the genocide.

Warnings Ignored

When the truth comes out about something as horrible as the genocide in Rwanda, the world is quick to declare it an atrocity of great proportions, but before such an event occurs, the world is, unfortunately, just as quick to deny its possibility. Thus, while much sorrow over such an event may later be expressed, often little effort is made to prevent the event from occurring.

There were a great many warnings that the genocide would occur, but the people who could have stopped it chose to look the other way. One of the most dramatic of these warnings came through the force commander of the UN Assistance Mission to Rwanda (UNAMIR), Lt. Gen. Roméo Dallaire. Dallaire's mission was to assist the peace process between the government's FAR troops and the RPF to facilitate the enforcement of the Arusha Peace Accords. Dallaire had twenty-five hundred UN troops, but their UN mandate stated they could not fire weapons unless fired upon, and that made them somewhat ineffective and continually put Dallaire in a delicate position. He could save lives, but he couldn't stop the killing.

The Interahamwe—Death Squads

The longer he stayed in Rwanda, the more Dallaire began to doubt President Habyarimana's intentions to enforce the accords, and in January of 1994, he met with an informant, who explained the reason to him. The man, code-named Jean-Pierre, said he had been an officer in the Presidential Guard, but had left the army to become the chief trainer for the Interahamwe. His direct superior was Mathieu Ngirumpatse, the president of the MRND party, who paid him a salary of 150,000 Rwandan francs a month (about $1,500 at the time).

In 1993, Jean-Pierre began teaching small groups of young men in the villages with a designated purpose to develop a local militia to fight the RPF if they attacked. In late 1993, however, the real plan behind the training of the Interahamwe was revealed. He was ordered to gather lists of Tutsis living in the villages under his designation, and he now suspected these lists were being made so the people on them could later be killed.

Jean-Pierre said that although he hated the RPF and saw them as Rwanda's enemy, he was horrified that he had become part of a plan to create a group of highly efficient death squads. He maintained that the death squads could kill a thousand Tutsis in Kigali in twenty minutes or less, if given the order. The Interahamwe were trained by army instructors at bases in several locations around the country. Every week more young men were brought in to receive a three-week course on the use of weapons and killing techniques. When their training was finished, the young men were returned to their villages and ordered to make lists of Tutsis until they were called into action.

Knowing that Dallaire would doubt the authenticity of such a wild story, Jean-Pierre revealed that he had helped organize recent demonstrations that the UN commander had witnessed. He said that the violent demonstrations were designed to provoke the UN's Belgian troops, which Dallaire had already suspected. Certain people were assigned the job of threatening the Belgians with clubs and machetes in an effort to push them into firing warning shots. If the shots had been fired, members of the Presidential Guard and others mingling in the crowd would have uncovered hidden firearms and begun an assault with the singular goal of killing as many Belgian soldiers as possible.

The UN's Response

Alarmed, Roméo Dallaire did what any good commander would do. He contacted his superiors at the UN. Their response, as described in Dallaire's book, *Shake Hands with the Devil: The Failure of Humanity in Rwanda,* was a portent of what was to come in Rwanda:

> The code cable from Kofi Annan . . . came to me and . . . its contents caught me completely off guard. It took me to task for even thinking about raiding the weapons caches and ordered me to suspend the operation immediately. Annan spelled out in excruciating detail the limits New York was placing upon me as force commander of a chapter-six peacekeeping operation; not only was I not allowed to conduct deterrent operations in support of UNAMIR, but in the interests of transparency, I was to provide the information that Jean-Pierre had given to us to President Habyarimana immediately. I was absolutely beside myself with frustration . . . For the rest of the week, I made phone call after phone call to New York, arguing . . . over the necessity of raiding the arms caches. During these . . . exchanges, I got the feeling that New York now saw me as a loose cannon and not as an aggressive but careful force commander.[5]

Frustrated and hoping additional proof would help his case, Dallaire followed Jean-Pierre's instructions and raided one of the hidden weapons caches. "The cache was in the basement of the headquarters of the MRND . . . [and] consisted of at least fifty assault rifles, boxes of ammunition, clips and grenades."[6]

Despite this new information, the UN refused to budge, and Dallaire lost contact with Jean-Pierre near the end of January. Perhaps he had escaped on his own or perhaps he was uncovered and executed. There were other warnings. Many human rights groups warned the international community of impending calamity in Rwanda, and by the end of March, most of them had evacuated their families from Kigali.

Chatter

In the early part of 1994, articles appeared in *Kangura* by CDR extremist Hassan Ngeze that claimed President Habyarimana would die in March at the hands of Hutus. Then, as the genocide grew closer, there was a lot of talk about "something very big coming in March." The clearest of such clues came in the form of a puzzling broadcast by RTLMC late on the third of April, which stated: "On the third, fourth and fifth, heads will get heated up. On 6 April, there will be a respite, but a little thing might happen. Then on the seventh and the eighth and the other days in April, you will see something."

Although there seems to be no discernable pattern, it is obvious that some people were warned in advance. In *La Libre Belgique,* Jean Birara said in an interview that an officer friend told him that "very serious things were in the making" and that he did not know whether "he would still be alive in a week's time."

Lighting the Fuse

By April, many Hutu extremists had said publicly that they felt President Habyarimana had betrayed them by signing the Arusha Peace Accords. Privately, the president told them he wasn't going to enforce the agreement, but they could see the mounting pressure on him to do so. There was little question that he was stalling on implementing the final solution. The killing squads had been trained, the weapons hidden at key places throughout the country, and large pits had been dug to conceal the bodies in the foolish belief that such an incredible crime could be concealed.

But the order had not been given. The president kept telling his fellow *genocidaires* that he needed more time, but it was clear to them that he was having doubts. Then Habyarimana was asked to come to Dar es Salaam in Tanzania to meet with other African leaders, supposedly to discuss the turmoil in Burundi. But the insiders knew that part of the purpose for this meeting was for the leaders to gang up on Habyarimana and demand to know why he was stalling on enforcing the Arusha Accords.

The Hutu extremists, especially those of the *akazu* knew that their position was at risk. What if Habyarimana was pressured enough that he would try to go ahead with the accords? They had to act.

In retrospect, it is likely that the genocide planners knew for some time that they needed a big event to shock the peasants into supporting the killing squads. Something that would fuel the madness of genocide, something they could later claim was the result of the spontaneous anger of the people. So, while Habyarimana met with President Ali Hassan Mwinyi of Tanzania, Vice President George Saitoti of Kenya, Cyprien Ntaryamira of Burundi, and President Yoweri Museveni of Uganda in Dar es Salaam, an even more significant meeting was going on in a clandestine room in Kigali. The decision was made. The signal would be given.

No doubt Habyarimana was tired after the meeting. With Uganda's President Museveni leading the way, much pressure was put on him to do what he had promised at Arusha. Even fellow Hutu Ntaryamira said Habyarimana's delay was endangering the security of Burundi. The criticism of these African leaders was underscored by implied threats. These were dangerous men, and Habyarimana could not afford their mutual displeasure for long.

He must have felt relieved to see the presidential jet waiting for takeoff. The *Falcon 50* was only four years old, a gift from President François Mitterrand of France, complete with a three-man French crew. At the airport President Ntaryamira admitted that he too was tired and asked Habyarimana for a ride.

Ntaryamira's plane, a propeller-driven aircraft, was much slower. It was decided that they would fly to Kigali first, and after dropping Habyarimana off, the plane would take President Ntaryamira to Bujumbura.

As they came in low to land at Kigali around 8:30 p.m. on April 6, 1994, two missiles were fired from just outside the airport's perimeter. The aircraft took a direct hit and exploded instantly, crashing ironically into the garden of Habyarimana's house in a ball of fire, killing everyone on board. The signal had been given.

The Coming of the Devil

Who shot down the president's plane? Within minutes of the crash, the extremist radio station, RTMLC, was announcing that the deed had been done by Tutsi extremists and that it was time to rid Rwanda of the Tutsi traitors—every man, woman, and child must be killed. Of course, the Tutsis, even those with some degree of money or power, had no missile-launching capabilities. The RPF had nothing of this kind anywhere near the capital.

In fact, the only people who had a missile launcher anywhere close to the airport were the government forces. The RGF, the government army, claimed they had no missile capability, but there were French antiaircraft guns and an unreported number of SA-7 missiles at their disposal located at the airport. The question has been raised that the RGF may not have had anyone capable of firing the missile launchers. Eyewitnesses have claimed that they saw French soldiers near the missile launchers on the night of April 6, but they could have been trainers or imported mercenaries brought in just for this purpose.

The men thought to have fired the missiles were seen by several eyewitnesses driving off from Masaka Hill minutes after the plane crash, and they were described as being white. While no one saw them fire the missiles, the fact that they were in an extreme hurry to leave the site where the missiles were fired has made them the primary suspects.

Belgian journalist Colette Braeckman wrote that Habyarimana's plane had been shot down by two French soldiers of the *Detachement d'Assistance*

Militaire et de l'Instruction (DAMI), the remnants of the French military structure that had not been completely dismantled when they left in December 1993. Braeckman claimed that the Belgian commission of inquiry agreed with her sources, but the results of their investigation have never been revealed to the public.

Crash Controversy

Since the shooting down of Habyarimana's plane directly led to launching the genocide that resulted in more than a million deaths, it is a subject that continues to inspire controversy to this very day, nearly a dozen years after the event. Recently a book by former RPF defector Abdul Ruzibiza was published in France, entitled *Rwanda: L'histoire secrète.*

Ruzibiza claims he was a lieutenant in the RPF who was part of a "network commando" that shot down the plane. The book claims that the RPF trans-ported SA-16 missiles from a Ugandan arsenal and smuggled them into Kigali by tricking the Ghanaian contingent of UN peacekeepers. The book maintains that the RPF then immediately launched a wave of attacks after the president's death. Not surprisingly, it then indirectly blames the RPF for the genocide and goes on to list other atrocities that it claims the RPF committed.

Ruzibiza's account runs contrary to every other description of what hap-pened at the Kigali airport on the night of April 6, 1994. Gen. Roméo Dallaire claims the RPF could not have had missiles at Kigali airport and that it is ludicrous to think something like this could have happened under the very noses of both the UN and Rwandan government troops that were stationed at that location.

The truth was, contrary to preparing for an attack, Paul Kagame and six hundred of his men were actually trapped in Kigali, behind enemy lines and separated from the main body of their troops. They were clearly caught off guard by the attack on the president's plane, and their counterattack did not begin until the genocide commenced.

Upon further investigation, it was learned that Ruzibiza only worked with the RPF as a nurse, and the RPF chief of staff claimed that he was placed in a mental hospital and then sentenced to prison for offenses he had committed. According to the chief of staff, Ruzibiza initially wrote a letter making the same type of claims to seek release from prison. Later, after he served his time and was released, he found someone to champion his cause. Not surprisingly, since the book was published in France, it alleviates the French of any responsibility for the genocide.

Habyarimana's plane was shot down by missiles that could only have come from launchers within an area controlled by the government's GP (*Garde Presidentielle* or President's Guard) forces and French soldiers. Immediately after the crash, the GP stood guard around the wreck of the *Falcon 50* for several days, preventing the experts from examining it. France's minister of cooperation, Michel Roussin, had to personally intervene three times to recover the bodies of the French three-man crew. Eventually the black box recording the last transmissions of the crew was given to French soldiers and taken to France. At one point the UN requested it, and the French refused to give it to them. It was finally released more than two years after the crash.

What the world press learned about the plane crash was what France chose to release to CNN. Rwanda had no means of controlling the press, but the superpowers did, and they sometimes released information to the news media in a very specific way. Even if someone in Rwanda did have the means to communicate to the world the truth about what was happening, the world would still believe a white television reporter before it believed a black man from Africa.

Fixing the Blame

The genocide planners knew that if the president was killed, they could blame it on the Tutsis and have the spark they needed to launch the genocide. At the same time, they could eliminate any responsibility for the planning and preparation of it, because they could blame it all on the dead president. They could say he planned it and that after he was killed the people carried it out. It would be chaos with no one to blame.

Indeed, part of the difficulty in affixing blame for the Rwandan genocide is that it became more about group psychology than a single villain. There were several people in the government who would do anything in order to maintain their power. There were numerous planners and countless evildoers, but no Hitler-type figure emerges as the main force behind the crime. If one had to name a general organizer of the whole operation, it would probably have to be Col. Théoneste Bagosora, the director of services in the Ministry of Defense.

Bagosora was a Hutu extremist who claimed he would one day "launch an apocalypse against the Tutsi." He was the behind-the-scenes creator of the "provisional government," and it was Bagosora who coordinated the "final solution," at least in the beginning stages. In the latter stages, there was such madness that the only force truly in control would have to have been the devil.

Next to Bagosora in terms of initial responsibility would probably be Maj. Gen. Augustin Bizimana, the defense minister who oversaw the logistics of the plan. One should also mention Jean Kambanda, who later became prime minister of the provisional government and was very prominent in inciting violence.

General Dallaire may have had a brief view behind the veil when he approached Bagosora after Habyarimana's death in an attempt to help restore order to the government. Deogratias Nsabimana, the chief of staff of the army, described how the president's plane had crashed:

> He began to smile as he told us that the plane had crashed in the backyard of Habyarimana's own home near Camp Kanombe, but caught himself. Bagosora gave him a dirty look, then turned to me for a response. I didn't even pause to offer condolences. I stressed that as far as UNAMIR and the world were concerned, Rwanda still had a government, headed by Prime Minister Agathe [Uwilingiyimana]. All matters should now be under her control. Bagosora snapped back that Madame Agathe didn't enjoy the confidence of the Rwandan people and was incapable of governing the nation. This Crisis Committee had to assume control until a new group of politicians could form a government. He had summoned the senior military leadership of the RGF to meet the next morning in Kigali. [7]

Perhaps the greatest argument that the government was behind the assassination of President Habyarimana is that the killing squads were on the streets less than two hours after the crash. As soon as Radio RTLMC announced the prearranged signal, the GP and the Interahamwe went into action, setting up roadblocks and eliminating Tutsis wherever they found them. The GP had about fifteen hundred men in Kigali, but they immediately called for help from the Interahamwe and Impuzamugambi—a militia that grew out of the CDR, a radical Hutu racist party. The Impuzamugambi had been created for just this moment.

The UN peacekeepers were caught in the middle. They repeatedly had been told by their superiors not to use force of any kind except to save themselves. They were not allowed to fire their weapons unless fired upon. General Dalliare found himself in a hostile situation, with no ability to take action. He and his men spent the first days of the genocide shuffling back and forth between the people now in charge of the government and making feeble attempts here and there to protect the innocent people they saw being slaughtered on the streets.

They soon realized that everything Jean-Pierre, their informant, had told them was coming to pass. The weapons had been taken out of their hiding places. "Each soldier carried an RF4 assault rifle," Dalliere reported. "[It was a weapon we] had never seen before in the hands of a Rwandan government soldier. The rifles were brand new, some with the packing grease still on the barrels." [8]

First Victims

The first victims of the genocide had been carefully chosen. They were the influential Tutsis and moderate Hutus—those with political power, money, or position, and who might be able to help any resistance. Most of them were killed the first day. Among them was the prime minister, Agathe Uwilingiyimana, a Hutu moderate. Viewing her as the logical voice of peace, General Dallaire tried to make arrangements for her to address the nation on the radio, but the station manager feared for his family if he agreed.

Fearful for the prime minister's safety, General Dallaire assigned ten Belgian soldiers from the UNAMIR to protect her. When the GP (Presidential Guard) surrounded her villa, they requested that the Belgians lay down their weapons. The men, who were privates without a commanding officer present, did what they thought was in keeping with their United Nations peacekeeping mandate and complied. The GP forces then escorted the Belgians to a nearby military camp, where they were killed. The prime minister was killed in her house; her five children only managed to survive through the help of neighbors.

When he lost contact with his men, Dallaire led a squad to Madame Agathe's home.

As the gate closed behind us, a rush of fifteen to twenty civilians appeared, all speaking at once. Captain Mbaye got them to calm down and then described for me the morning's horrible events. He had made his own way here from the Hotel des Mille Collines as word had filtered in about Madame Agathe from civilians seeking shelter there. By the time he got [there] the prime minister and her husband had been captured by men from the Presidential Guard and the army. They had surrendered in order to save their children, who were still hiding. Madame Agathe and her husband were murdered on the spot; there was blood on the wall and signs of grenade explosions at the entrance of one house as well as in the living room.[9]

When Dallaire pressed for information about his men, the government troops told him they were at the hospital. When he arrived there, he was taken to a courtyard near the morgue.

At first, I saw what seemed to be sacks of potatoes to the right of the morgue door. It slowly resolved in my vision into a heap of mangled and bloodied white flesh in tattered Belgian para-commando uniforms. The men were piled on top of each other, and we couldn't tell how many were in the pile. The light was faint and it was hard to identify any of the faces or find specific markings. We counted them twice: eleven soldiers. In the end it turned out to be ten.[10]

Dallaire began his mad shuffle back and forth between the government and the RPF, which was now planning a full-scale attack. At the Hotel des Mille Collines, immortalized as "Hotel Rwanda" by the film of the same name, Dallaire got another glimpse into the gravity of the situation.

> The lobby, patio and rooms were filled with terrified civilians, who crowded around me begging for information and protection. I told them all to remain calm and tried to be encouraging, but words were all I could offer. I was discreetly trying to spot Captain Mbaye when he appeared out of nowhere and pulled me aside . . . he had gathered Prime Minister Agathe's children, put them under a pile of clothes in the back of his vehicle and driven them to the hotel . . . I told him I would do what I could to get them out. Without a doubt, there would be informers in the hotel—he was to keep the kids hidden in the room.[11]

It was the same story across the city. Within thirty-six hours of the president's plane crash, which signaled the start of the genocide, most of the prominent Tutsis in the capital were dead. Joseph Kavaruganda, the president of the constitutional court, was killed, partly because of his liberal political views and partly because the constitutional succession to power after the president's death would then be nearly impossible to enforce.

Casualties and Survivors

Boniface Ngulinzira, former foreign minister and a chief negotiator of the Arusha agreement, was murdered, as was Faustin Rocogoza, the information minister. Minister of Agriculture Frederic Nzamurambaho, also director of a rival political party (the PSD), was killed, as was his assistant, Théoneste Gafaranga, and several of their party comrades, nearly wiping out the PSD leadership. The leader of the democratic fraction of the *Parti Liberal*, Landwald Ndasingwa, was killed along with his Canadian wife and their two children. Andre Kamweya, the journalist whose newspaper *Rwanda Rushya* was particularly hated by the extremists, was murdered, as was Charles Shamukiga, civil rights activist and businessman.

Some escaped death, including Monique Mujawamaliya, the civil rights activist who hid in the ceiling of her house until the killers left and then managed to leave the country. Marc Ruganera, the minister of finance and his colleagues, Joseph Ngarambe and Sylvestre Rwibajige, also escaped. The squad of killers who murdered the prime minister were assigned to kill her successor, Faustin Twagiramungu, but went to the house next to his, allowing him time to escape over the garden fence and later find sanctuary with the UN forces.

Moderate Hutus and anyone known to sympathize with the Tutsis were also killed. Many journalists were killed because they had written openly about corruption among those in power. Several priests and nuns were killed because they tried to stop militiamen from killing others. The priests at the Christus Center and their cook were killed simply because they were known to support the democratic transition in the government.

Quite a few people were murdered simply because of their social class. People were killed because they owned a car, or were well dressed or spoke good French, and were not known as government party supporters. Their money or marks of social distinction made them suspects. In Kigali the Interahamwe had tended to recruit mostly among the poor, although the camaraderie, the numerous material advantages, and even a form of political ideal also made them attractive to some middle-class young people.

Bizarre, but Deadly as Devils

Bizarrely dressed in cotton combat fatigues covered with strange symbols painted in the red, green, and black of the Rwandan flag, and carrying machetes or carved replicas of Kalashnikov rifles, the Interahamwe looked and acted like clowns, but they were as deadly as devils. Once they began the killing in Kigali, they drew around them a group of even poorer people, the homeless—street boys, car washers, and rag pickers. They saw the genocide as a blessing that allowed them to take revenge on the wealthy and powerful, providing their victims were in opposition to the Hutu extremists. They could rape, steal, and even kill with little or no justification, and they could get drunk for free. These people had little or no political goals—they simply went along for the ride.

Though it wasn't intended, the end result was little if any difference between ethnic and social criteria for the murders in Kigali. The Tutsis in the capital tended to be better off financially than the Hutus. Although the political power had been with the Hutus for thirty-five years, the educational and social aspects of the Belgian favoritism toward the Tutsis for the previous forty years was still paying off.

Tutsis held most of the jobs in the foreign embassies and international agencies, and there were still many successful Tutsi businessmen. Even the high-priced call girls in the big hotels were Tutsis. The Interahamwe were fueled far more by social envy than political rivalry. Gen. Roméo Dallaire described the turmoil in the streets:

> Reports were coming in from all over the city that all the major intersections were blocked. Brent [Major Brent Beardsley] took a UN bus and a local driver to collect some of our civilian staff who had agreed to work that Saturday morning. At one location he found a man with a severe machete wound and took him to the hospital. But no amount of negotiation could secure safe passage for the bus carrying our civilian staff through the mobs. Brent decided to drop the staff off at the Meridien, and then took a circuitous route back to the Amahoro, only to come upon a man and a woman being hauled from a vehicle by another mob. Captain Claeys also happened to be driving by, and he stopped too. Brent, Claeys, and Troute rushed the mob and everyone ran, leaving the couple behind. They turned out to be a Tutsi doctor and his wife, a nurse, who had been trying to get to the Kigali hospital, as the radio was alleging that there were large numbers of casualties throughout the city. [12]

By midday on April 7, the killers were going house to house looking for Tutsis. Most they murdered wherever they found them, in their homes or on the street. Some they carried away to a mass grave near the airport, where they cut off their arms and legs and dumped them into the pit. Horrified by what he was seeing, General Dallaire cabled New York asking for more troops. Dallaire believed he could stop the genocide if he had five thousand troops and permission for them to use their weapons. He already had twenty-five hundred men, and the rest could have been on the ground in Rwanda in a day or two. But the UN administration in New York delayed answering. Analysts today agree that fulfilling Dallaire's request would have stopped the genocide and probably saved a million lives.

Massacres in the Churches

Perhaps the most horrifying aspect of the Rwandan genocide was the killing of thousands and thousands of innocent men, women, and children that took place in the churches. During previous persecutions the Tutsis had often sought and been granted sanctuary in the churches. Since the government's plan for the 1994 genocide was to leave no Tutsi alive, it had been decided early by the *genocidaires* to attack the churches as part of the massacre. In a truly macabre and sacrilegious twist, the genocide planners convinced numerous pastors and religious leaders to join their plot. The clergymen were to encourage Tutsis to seek sanctuary in their churches; they would then notify the government death squads to perform the slaughter.

Only those clergy thought to be sympathetic with the extremists were informed; many others had no idea their congregations would be massacred in their houses of worship. Dallaire describes the killing in one church in Kigali:

> In the aisles and on the pews were bodies of hundreds of men, women, and children. At least fifteen of them were still alive but in a terrible state. The priests were applying first aid to the survivors. A baby cried as it tried to feed on the breast of its dead mother . . . the two Polish MILOBs . . . were in a state of grief and shock, hardly able to relate what had happened. The night before,

they said, the RGF had cordoned off the area, and then the Gendarmerie had gone door to door checking identity cards. All Tutsi men, women, and children were rounded up and moved to the church . . .

Then the gendarmes welcomed in a large number of civilian militiamen with machetes and handed over the victims to their killers. Methodically and with much bravado and laughter, the militia moved from bench to bench, hacking with machetes. Some people died immediately, while others with terrible wounds begged for their lives or the lives of their children. No one was spared. A pregnant woman was disembowelled and her fetus severed. Women suffered horrible mutilation. Men were struck on the head and died immediately or lingered in agony. Children begged for their lives and received the same treatment as their parents. Genitalia were a favourite target, the victims left to bleed to death. There was no mercy, no hesitation and no compassion. The priests and the MILOBs, guns at their throats, tears in their eyes, and the screams of the dying in their ears, pleaded with the gendarmes for the victims. The gendarmes' reply was to use the rifle barrels to lift the priests' and MILOBs' heads so that they could better witness the horror. [13]

In many places the local church was a deathtrap. Sometimes the priests pleaded for the lives of the people, and in some cases they were killed for it. But, in most churches, the Interahamwe simply came and killed masses of Tutsi people. If the number of people proved to be too much for them to handle, they called on the army to launch mortar shells through the roof or throw hand grenades through the windows to flush the people out. Sometimes the killing took several days. Killing someone with a machete is not always easy. Often the death squads would grow tired at the end of the day and would cut the Achilles tendons of anyone still left alive, so their gruesome work could begin again in the morning.

The reaction of the clergy during the genocide crossed all lines and extremes ranging from Hutu pastors who died for their Tutsi congregations to those who actually participated in the murders. A Roman Catholic priest at Nyange hired a caterpillar to bulldoze the church on top of the bodies of his congregation, and two Benedictine nuns were convicted of supplying the gasoline used to burn down a garage sheltering five hundred Tutsi refugees next to their church.

The failures and successes of the Rwandan clergy to live up to their faith will be discussed in detail in the section focusing on the village massacres, but those failures resulted in some of the most bizarre and tragic scenes in the entire genocide, and must rank among the worst acts of mankind.

Atrocities in Hospitals and Schools

Any type of business, organization, or building that housed a large number of Tutsis was the scene of atrocities during the genocide. In the hospitals, squads of gun and machete-brandishing killers regularly stormed through the halls, assuming that anyone who was wounded was a Tutsi and killing them on the spot. Dallaire recalled:

> Right in front of our eyes, the army men would come inside the hospital, take the wounded, line them up and machine-gun them down . . . It was also the first time in any of our operations that we saw our local personnel being killed on a massive scale. All our Tutsi medical staff, doctors and nurses, were kidnapped and murdered in Kigali in April. Over two hundred people. We had never seen anything like it.[14]

There was also the case of Andre Rwamakuba, the former minister for primary and secondary education in the interim government during 1994, and a member of MDR. The International Criminal Tribunal for Rwanda (ICTR) tried Rwamakuba for allegedly checking the identities of patients at the National University hospital in Butare and ordering Tutsi patients to be taken away; they were never seen again. Rwamakuba was also accused of leading massacres on the hospital premises. According to his indictment, he beat wounded patients to death with clubs and allowed the Interahamwe militiamen accompanying him to kill women and to remove the insides from those who were pregnant.

Conditions in the hospitals were awful. Doctors and nurses were severely overworked, and the war was a constant threat. Red Cross and other medical workers were not immune to the slaughter. More than fifty Rwandans working for the Red Cross were killed during the conflict, and even some white nurses and doctors were injured. Emergency vehicles were often stopped and checked, and hundreds of Tutsi casualties were pulled from ambulances and killed. Dallaire described one such scenario that also provides a startling portrait of the youth of the Interahamwe:

> On one trip to the city centre, I saw a white Red Cross van, angled on the road, riddled with bullet holes. Smoke was coming out of the engine compartment and all the windows were smashed. The passenger door was open and a Rwandan in a Red Cross vest was hanging down, facing us, with blood oozing from his head in a slow, steady stream. The back doors were open and a body on a stretcher was still inside, with another held up on the bumper. There were three other casualties, their white and bloodied gauze dressings spun around them. One body had no head. Five blood-spattered youths sat on the curb, smoking cigarettes beside the ambulance. Their machetes were stained red. At most they may have been fifteen years old.[15]

Philippe Gaillard, the leader of the Red Cross's efforts in Rwanda, took the bold step of going public about the Red Cross being hindered from saving lives, even though he knew this would put his life in danger. "In such circumstances, if you don't speak out clearly, you are participating," Gaillard later told a PBS *Frontline* documentary. "Morally, ethically you cannot shut up."[16]

After the publicity surrounding Gaillard's statement, the attacks on the Red Cross and hospitals lessened considerably. The situation in the schools was no better than in the hospitals or churches. At the Don Bosco school, Belgian UNAMIR soldiers protected two thousand Tutsis, but on April 11, when the UN soldiers were ordered to withdraw to the airport, most of the civilians they abandoned were killed. There were also many instances of Hutu teachers denouncing their Tutsi pupils to the militia or even killing them. If you were Tutsi, there were no places of refuge in Rwanda.

The Madness Spreads

By the second day, the madness had spread to other major cities. In Gisenyi, a tourist town on Lake Kivu, survivors reported a festive spirit on the part of the killers, who joyfully cut down men, women, and children in the streets. In Kibungo, government soldiers were killing every Tutsi and Hutu moderate they found and burning their homes. Meanwhile things were so bad in Kigali that bulldozers were digging deeper trenches at the roadblocks to handle the piles of bodies. All along the main thoroughfares there were prisoners in their pink jail uniforms, sent out for roadwork duty, picking up corpses and throwing them into dump trucks to be hauled away.

They killed you if your identity card said you were a Tutsi, they killed you if your identity card said you were a Hutu but you looked like a Tutsi, and they killed you if you didn't have an identity card. Sometimes, if they knew you were mixed, then they expected you to show that you were a "true Hutu" by your actions toward the Tutsi. There were many who came from mixed families that did atrocious things to Tutsis, thinking it would help them survive.

The goal was to kill every Tutsi in Rwanda. While the government knew there were hundreds of thousands of Tutsis in other countries, they believed that if they murdered every Tutsi in Rwanda, the exiles would never dare come back or, for that matter, even have a reason to come back, because there would be no one alive to find. In many cases they went as far as destroying the victims' identity cards and public records at the local commune office, which effectively erased many of these people from existence.

And they had a plan to antagonize the situation for Tutsis in other parts of Africa, especially Uganda, Burundi, Tanzania, and the Congo. They planned to launch the propaganda program in those countries as well. In Burundi they were already telling the people that the Tutsis killed their president by shooting down Habyarimana's plane. Many people there were already saying that the Tutsi guerrillas had killed their president, and therefore, all the Tutsis had to die.

Evacuating the Whites

While the international community debated whether there was genocide happening in Rwanda, they decided en masse to get their people out of the country. French soldiers arrived in Kigali to assist in the evacuation. On Tuesday, April 12, the French ambassador to Rwanda, Jean-Philippe Marlaud, closed the embassy and left to join planeloads of departing bureaucrats.

All the embassies were closed, and the majority of the white people left. Exceptions were a handful of missionaries and humanitarian workers such as Marc Vaiter, who somehow kept his orphanage open during the siege of Kigali, and Carl Wilkens, an aid worker with the Adventist Church. There were probably fewer than thirty white people left in the entire country. This made things even easier for the *genocidaires,* who could now kill without the worry of prying Western eyes. Left behind were the Rwandan people who worked at those embassies or for the white-run businesses. Some of them were Tutsis who many times had shown their loyalty in the midst of adversity. But the loyalty was not returned, and now they were doomed.

General Dallaire, whose forces were cut from 2,500 to 250 men after the murder of the Belgian soldiers guarding the prime minister, remembered:

> I passed by an assembly point where French soldiers were loading expatriates into vehicles. Hundreds of Rwandans had gathered to watch all these white entrepreneurs, NGO staff and their families making their fearful exits, and as I wended my way through the crowd, I saw how aggressively the French were pushing black Rwandans seeking asylum out of the way. A sense of shame overcame me. The whites, who had made their money in Rwanda and who had hired so many Rwandans to be their servants and labourers, were now abandoning them. Self-interest and self-preservation ruled.[17]

The hurried evacuation was pitiful. Some Americans, like Laura Lane, from the United States Embassy in Kigali, had tried to smuggle Tutsis out in their entourage, but few made it. At every roadblock, scared Tutsis riding the trucks were pulled off the vehicles and slaughtered under the noses of the French soldiers, who, obeying their mandate, made no move to stop it. French dignitaries heavily involved with the Habyarimana government were running for cover while the Tutsis who worked for them were abandoned to their deaths.

Mixed-race couples were not even allowed on board. Everywhere there were families being split apart—whites with Tutsi spouses were forced to leave them behind. White mothers had to cry and beg to take their half-Tutsi children with them.

Hotel Rwanda

The situation at the Hotel des Mille Collines was getting worse by the day. Paul Rusesabagina, the hotel manager, by now had taken in hundreds of Tutsi refugees. Several times government troops, and even the Interahamwe, had come to the hotel to take them, but each time Rusesabagina had managed to bribe the killers to move on or delay them long enough to get help. He remembered that when the hotel acquired a fax machine, an auxiliary telephone line was installed to support it. When the phones to the hotel were cut off, Rusesabagina discovered that the old fax line still had a dial tone. It was this line that he used to get help.

"We could ring the king of Belgium," Rusesabagina said. "I could get through to the Ministry of Foreign Affairs of France immediately. We sent many faxes to Bill Clinton himself at the White House." Rusesabagina would often stay up until four in the morning "sending faxes, calling, ringing the whole world." The Hutu Power leaders in Kigali suspected he had a phone, but "they never had my number, so they didn't know how to cut it off."

RPF Advances

As soon as the genocide began, the RPF started advancing from the positions they had held at the time of the Arusha Accords cease-fire. Kagame informed the UNAMIR that he was going to move his six hundred troops, along with a number of Tutsi refugees, out of the capital in the dark of night.

"What Brent and I were witnessing was the movement of over twelve thousand people of all ages in the dark in order not to draw RGF fire," UNAMIR Commander Dallaire recalled. "It was like a parade of ghosts, heads bowed, burdened with their few possessions, moving in the dark of night to an unknown destination where at least they would be safe." [18]

Dallaire had gained respect for the RPF through his frequent negotiations with Kagame and upon witnessing the discipline of the troops. In *Shake Hands with the Devil,* he wrote:

> After evening prayers, I had a cup of tea with Faustin [prime minister designate Faustin Twagiramungu] in my office. His family hadn't yet been located and he had again spent most of the day listening to the propaganda being broadcast by RTLM—a stream of commentators were exhorting violence, playing provocative songs and even reading out the names and locations of those who must be killed . . . Faustin thought that the RPF would win this war. Its soldiers were fighting for a cause they believed in, whereas the RGF soldiers were killing for the sake of killing, not knowing or caring why. In this type of conflict, the men fighting for principles they believed in would inevitably win. [19]

The Demons Unleashed

Radio-Coordinated Attacks

The day after the attacks began in Kigali, the Interahamwe went from village to village, slaughtering men, women, and children. Rarely was there any resistance, but if so, they simply radioed for government soldiers, who were always nearby. The killers were often brought to the villages in government trucks; the bodies were carried away in those same trucks, to be buried in huge pits the government had dug for just that purpose. Sometimes the bodies were thrown in the river. Sometimes they were hacked to pieces, and those pieces were stacked just outside the village like firewood—a stack of arms here, a stack of legs or heads there.

The death squads carried small radios and listened constantly to station RTLMC for directions. The radio station had given the signal for the attacks to begin, and it coordinated the action, letting the killers know what villages had been overlooked or where a "nest" of Tutsi survivors might be hiding. Although much of Rwanda is gardenlike open country, its many mountains provide so many nooks and crannies that it took a considerable amount of organization to make sure every place was checked.

In each village the local Hutu populace was pressed into service because only they would know the hiding places in their village. No matter how well a person hid, someone in the village would probably see him or her. If someone tried to run away, someone else would know what direction that person went. There were just too many people involved in the hunt. Only the most cunning and careful survived. And even in those cases, the ones who got away usually experienced some kind of miracle—inside help or a very lucky break.

The killers had been preparing for a long time. They had lists of names and maps showing where the Tutsis lived, and they also knew which Hutus might give them trouble. The instructions were clear: if any Hutu raised a hand to stop the slaughter—no matter if it was to save his neighbor, wife, or child—that one, too, would be killed on the spot. Everywhere, in every village, there were massacres.

One reason the death toll was so high was that many people in the villages simply refused to believe that such a thing was really happening. There had been massacres before, but never anything like this—a thorough and detailed elimination of Tutsi men, women, and children. Many people heard it on the radio and simply did not believe it.

The RPF radio station, Mahavoro, was also broadcasting at this time, telling the people about the genocide. The station told them that all Tutsis were being executed, and they needed to flee for their lives. But still people stayed. In many cases, those who did believe it were too scared even to leave their houses. They thought they would be safer in their homes than on the road. It's human nature to think that way, but eventually the killers came and murdered them right there in their houses.

There were some places the RPF warned the people, saying, "They are going to kill you. Run! Get out of there!"

And these people replied, "Yes. We hear you, but where do we go? There are roadblocks everywhere. Maybe I will get lucky here." But very few survived.

Mugisozi: Javan Sebasore's Story

Javan Sebasore described the attack on the village of Mugisozi:

The attack started on the seventh of April when the president's plane was shot down. My wife and I were living near Nyarutovu but we had gone to Mugisozi to visit my in-laws. We arrived on the sixth and were supposed to go back on the seventh. Then we heard that President Habyarimana had died in a plane crash . . . We were afraid because they had already been killing Tutsis here and there and we knew that the death of the president was going to make things a lot worse. Then about 10:20 in the morning someone came and told us they had began killing people in a neighborhood some distance away.[1]

As was the case in most areas, those in Sebasore's family simply didn't believe that such a thing could be happening.

We didn't believe him. We thought he was trying to deceive us so we would leave the house and he could come and loot it. We didn't trust him because he was one of the extremists and they were the ones who were supposed to be killing people. After a short while the man came back and said, "Be prepared. The group is coming." Some of us went to see and they saw a large and violent group coming with the guns, and grenades, and the clubs with nails in them. Then we became scared and the elders told us to run and try to save ourselves.[2]

As had been the case so often in the past, the people sought the sanctuary of the church.

There was an Adventist church and everybody tried to maneuver their way towards it . . . some of the killers ran to stop us, but I saw others motion to them. They said, "Let them go." And I thought maybe they are just going to let us run to the church so they can kill us all there and make the church a slaughterhouse.[3]

Javan's premonition was correct, and ultimately it would save his life.

We arrived in the church and many of the people started singing hymns. Then, trucks full of Interahamwe arrived. They were blowing whistles and chanting anti-Tutsi slogans. The church was full, over 300 people—men, women, and children. I began thinking that I should get out of the church. I am tall and knew that I would stand out in the crowd there and I just kept feeling I should leave, so finally I left and hid in a small building beside the church.[4]

Did God warn Javan Sebasore? And if so, was God trying to warn the others as well, but they were not able to hear through their fear? Or did God, in His infinite wisdom, have a plan and purpose in saving Javan Sebasore? Perhaps Javan was spared so he could tell his story:

I could hear everything from my hiding place. Around two a bigger group of Interahamwe arrived and when the people who were in the church saw them surrounding it, they closed the doors and the windows. I could hear the Interahamwe swearing and then they hit on the doors and windows and forced them open and started throwing grenades into the church. The grenades exploded and some fragments fell on top of the house I was hiding in. The Interahamwe began shooting into the windows and then they would shoot anyone who tried to leave the church. Then the people started calling out. "Havyaramanna, son of so and so, you are killing us." They knew them. Many of them were their neighbors. They would call out to their killers by name and say, "Why do you kill us?" The killers wouldn't stop but I heard them being called by name so I knew who was doing the killing. [5]

It was common belief that if a man was named, the blood of the person he was murdering would haunt him. So if a person heard his name called out, he would stop for a while and someone who had not been named would do the killing instead. That's what the organizers told them to do to avoid being haunted by the blood.

"It took them a whole hour to kill the people grouped inside the church," Sebasore recalled. "My sisters and cousins all ran to the church thinking it was the only place where they could survive. Instead it became a slaughter place for them.[6]

But the trial was not over for Javan.

At one point, I heard one of the killers say that he hadn't seen a tall man who was wearing a black jacket among the victims. And the pastor, who was a Hutu, said, "You have killed so many people. How could you recognize one dead body from among the 300 you have destroyed?" Then one of the men said, "But I didn't see the man in the black coat die. He must be hiding in the pastor's house." So they forced the pastor to open his house. It was getting late and he gave them a torch and said, "Search the house and look under the beds and look everywhere. I don't want you to come back and bother me later." The pastor knew where I was hiding, but he didn't take them there.[7]

Sebasore remembered that one man, in particular, was reluctant to give up the search.

Ndorayabo Eliab was the one who brought the killers to the church in his truck. He is now sentenced to death for his crimes. He was leading the search, forcing the pastor to look everywhere. He kept saying that the Tutsis did a bad thing by killing the president and therefore deserved death.

Eventually, they came to where I was hiding. One of the men entered the very room where I was hiding. He was wearing grenades around his belt and had a machete and a club. I thought then that I was definitely dead, because he would see me, but he came in and felt around in the darkness of the room . . . he touched my head, but then he went out without saying anything. It was during daylight, but when he came in from outside to the dark room his eyes did not see clearly.

But I could see clearly because I had been hiding in the dark room a long time and was used to the darkness . . . when he went out, I thought he would remove the pin on one of the grenades and throw it in to kill me. But instead he went on into another small house across from where I was. And then I heard him say, "There is nobody here. Let's go." I realized God had saved me.[8]

Later, after darkness fell, the pastor called out to him.

At first the pastor said he felt it was not wise for me to get out, because his children would see me and might talk about it. And I knew I had no strength to run. I hadn't had anything to drink or eat, so I decided to wait through the night. The next day on the eighth of April I stayed hid, but that night people came and told the pastor they were going to come to search his house again because they still hadn't found me.

They said, "We shall search your house and if we find him we will kill him and you will be punished." So that night the pastor came and told me, "You have to leave because I don't want you to be killed here." He gave me some food and clothes and a light. I told him I wanted to travel late at night when there were fewer people out. I told him I was going to go to my place of birth, which was toward the volcanic mountains. That night I escaped. Later, I saw that Hutu pastor in Uganda, and thanked him for saving my life.[9]

Nyirubuye: Valentina Iribagiza's Story

Valentina Iribagiza, a Tutsi schoolgirl, was seeking shelter at the Catholic Church at Nyirubuye on April 15, when villagers armed with machetes attacked those in the church. She survived by hiding under the bodies of those already slain. "I hid under dead people. The blood covered me so they thought they had killed me."

Later that night though, the killers came back to the church to sift through the bodies for survivors. Valentina told *Frontline:*

It was very late, around 2:00 AM, when the Interahamwe came back. One of them stepped on my head. He was shaking me . . . to see if I was alive. He said, "This thing is dead," and so they left. I lived among the dead for a long time. At night the dogs would come to eat the bodies. Once a dog was eating someone next to me. I threw something at [him] and he ran away. I hid in a small room. That's where I stayed and slept for 43 days.[10]

The Killings in the Villages

In every district across the country, the killing spread. In each village the local prefect followed instructions and gave the soldiers or Interahamwe complete access and assistance. There was only one place where a local government official provided any resistance. In Butare, Jean-Baptiste Habyarimana (no relation to the late president), the only Tutsi prefect left in power, refused to comply with the government's wishes. After Habyarimana held his ground for two weeks, and many Tutsis came to the region for sanctuary, the interim government president, Theodore Sindikubwabo, visited Butare on April 19, 1994. He fired the prefect (who was then killed) and denounced his "inaction."

In a speech broadcast throughout the country on RTLMC, the president asked the people if they were "sleeping" and urged them to violent deeds. On the twentieth, Habyarimana was replaced by Sylvain Ndikumana, a Hutu extremist, and members of the GP were flown down from Kigali by helicopter to join truckloads of militia to begin the massacre. Murder finally had its way in Butare, and the killings there included some of the worst massacres of the genocide. In Cyahinda parish, at least twenty thousand Tutsis were killed, and in Karama parish the number of deaths was closer to thirty-five thousand.

The killings in the villages included some of the worst atrocities man has ever committed against a fellow human being, especially considering that many of them were committed in churches. They were efficient and thorough in their scope and unimaginably cruel in their execution. The machete, which renders a long and painful death, was the primary weapon. Many people gave their killers what little money they had and begged for a bullet rather than face the hacking death of the *panga*.

The killers were particularly harsh with women and children. In fact, it often seemed that the more defenseless and innocent a person was, the more likely they were to suffer a terrible death. Women were not only raped; they were gang-raped. They were raped to death with objects—tree branches, knives, poles, and logs.

Children were shot, clubbed, chopped up, and strangled. Babies often had their heads smashed against the wall of the church or slammed into a rock. Breasts and penises were often chopped off. The killings sometimes resembled ritual mutilations akin to ancient sacrifices to the demon gods of pagan worship.

In Gisenyi province, a Hutu priest tried to protect two hundred children by hiding them in his church. As he prayed, the death squad pushed open the doors to the church and killed everyone inside, including him. In that same province a chapel was burned while hundreds of people screamed inside.

Special Umugandas

The massacres in the villages were usually preceded by a political meeting, during which the people were "educated" to the gravity of the Tutsi problem. Usually some important person from Kigali joined the local *bourgmestre* (mayor) or prefect to provide an even greater sense of official sanction. While designed to fire up the local peasants enough to kill, the meetings also desensitized them to the act of killing by using euphemisms and metaphors.

The meetings were referred to as a special *umuganda* (collective work session). The massacres were referred to as "bush clearing" or "weed pulling" and the slaughter of children as "pulling out the roots of the bad weeds." Tutsis in the village were denounced as potential collaborators with the RPF. They were the enemy and had to be exterminated for the safety and good of Rwanda. Often, the meetings were similar in tone to the propaganda broadcasts on Radio RTLMC.

The RPF were depicted as creatures from another world, with tails, horns, hooves, pointed ears, and red eyes that glowed in the dark. Naturally, anyone who was their accomplice was also likely to be a very evil creature. Most people in the villages were illiterate, and, given their authoritarian tradition, they tended to believe what the authorities told them. A prisoner interviewed at the prison in Ruhengiri described one such meeting:

When the president died a policeman came to Gisosi, our village, around seven in the morning the next day and told us we must kill the Tutsis. They said the

RPF killed the president and that they were killing Hutus everywhere they went and we must avenge their deaths. They said we must kill the Tutsi and destroy their properties. I said, "But these Tutsi have always lived here near us. We know them." But the policeman said we had to kill them.[11]

Sometimes the killing began as soon as the meeting was finished. Sometimes they waited for help from soldiers or Interahamwe. The order would come from the Ministry of the Interior in the capital or from the local prefect. Some *bourgmestres,* such as Remy Gatete in Kibungo and Fidele Rwambuka in Kanzenze, became widely known for the enthusiasm with which they killed, but others treated the murders with the same excitement they would any other order from Kigali. It was carried out with an unquestioned finality or even a solemn sense of patriotic duty.

Sometimes people would even apologize, telling their neighbors that they were sorry they had to kill them, but it was on orders from the government. The perpetrators of genocides are usually men of the herd, men who follow orders without questioning them. Rwanda was no exception.

Like those in Kigali, there was also a materialistic quality to the killings in the villages. The families being killed had land and sometimes cows and other possessions that provided excellent spoils to the killers. In overpopulated Rwanda, this was not a negligible incentive. The killers looted the households of their victims and slaughtered their cattle. Grand feasts were held to celebrate the massacres.

But greed was not the main motivation. It was belief and obedience— belief in the Tutsis' arrogant superiority that had been deeply planted so long ago by the Belgian masters, and obedience both to the political authority of the state and to the social authority of the group. Rwanda was known for its "culture of obedience." This was a government-encouraged activity. The authorities told them to do it. How could it be wrong?

Atrocities

Consequently, people in the villages completely gave themselves over to the killing in ways that would later horrify the rest of the world. They set fire to old women. They threw babies in the air and smashed them on the ground. They drowned people in the raw sewage of the latrine pits. They killed people they knew. They killed their neighbors.

In some villages the soldiers and Interahamwe arrived with big dump trucks. They herded the Tutsis onto the trucks and made them lie facedown. Then they piled logs of firewood on top of them. They stacked another row of Tutsis on top of that, and then more firewood, and so on until the truck was full. They drove the truck to a huge pit, either a natural one or one that they had dug, and dumped the people and the firewood into the pit.

People would be crushed and suffocated and then slide off the truck bed into the huge pit. They kept loading and dumping the trucks until the pit was full or there were no more Tutsis to kill in that area. Other times they just threw all the Tutsis into the village latrine and then dumped rocks and bricks on top of them until they were sure that they were all dead. A woman from the Ruhengiri province, who was still too fearful to give her name, told what happened to her father:

> It started in 1990 in our area. They took my father and my uncle and put them in a tipper truck like that. They put them on the floor and on top of them they put pieces of wood. Then they dropped them into a deep pit, a natural pit which we call *Enyaroconga,* an endless pit. There was a policeman who was among the team who took them into that pit. He had a small knife and he cut a finger off of my father's hand and he brought it to us to prove that he died. He said, "Don't look for him. This is the sign that he has been killed."[12]

Antoine Mupenzi recalled other atrocities: "Some pregnant women in our village died when they cut them open and took the babies from their stomach. They also put some people in big vats of cooking oil and cooked them alive."[13]

The horrors in the villages included all types of physical and mental torture and were marked by unnecessary cruelty. Often husbands were forced to kill their Tutsi wives or half-Tutsi children, before being killed. Any form of sympathy was grounds for death. My former pastor, a Hutu, was put in jail just because he visited his Tutsi in-laws after their houses were burned and some of them were killed. After that, even his own family did not visit him in jail. They abandoned him because of fear and the idea that he should never have been married to a Tutsi woman.

The killers who were known to have HIV were often assigned the task of raping the Tutsi women so they would become infected with the lethal virus. Afterward the women would be left alive for a few days, or even a week, to let the pain of that knowledge sink into their psyches before they were killed. Public humiliation was another form of torture practiced on the Tutsi women. The same woman from the Ruhengiri area told the story of two young Tutsi girls in her village during the carnage of 1994:

> One of the worst things that happened in our village was to a family of a man called Thomas. He was our neighbor and he had two beautiful daughters. They arrested them and they took them down to the main road on the highway. Then they gang raped them in the middle of the road. One by one, all the soldiers and the men with them raped them and then just left them there, naked in the road. They were unconscious and couldn't even move. Then some people, Hutus I think, who were merciful, came along and picked them up, covered them, and took them to the hospital. Then when they were beginning to recover and came home from the hospital, the same men came a second time and killed them. After having done such a horrible thing to them, they still came and killed them.[14]

This woman only survived because she and her husband hid in the bushes near their village. "One of the Christians, a Hutu, took our firstborn in and helped us in the bushes, bringing us food and giving us covers until the killers went away. I was breast-feeding my youngest, so I kept her with me."[15]

There is no greater pain for a parent than seeing his or her child killed, and this was not overlooked. The same woman described what happened to her sister: "My young sister had her first baby. When they came to her house to kill her family, she asked them to kill her first so she wouldn't have to see them kill her baby. They said, 'If you love your baby, then hold your baby well.' Then they shot the baby through the chest while she held it. They killed her on her lap. Then they killed my sister after they killed the child." [16]

At this point the woman broke down and cried for some time. Eleven years is not enough time for such pain to heal. "I cry a lot," she admitted, "especially when I remember my big happy family . . . There were seventy-four people in my family and only three of us survived. Many families were totally wiped out." [17]

The Devil in Rwanda

In many cases these horrible crimes were committed against people the perpetrators had known all their lives. People they had grown up with, gone to school with, whom they loved, and with whom they had shared life experiences. And they killed them in such terrible ways. Imagine raping someone in the middle of the road. Gang-raping two young girls in the middle of the road and stopping cars from both ways to have everyone watch and cheer the rapists on. That is the cruelty of all cruelty under the heavens.

Imagine shooting a baby in the chest while held in its mother's arms—the lungs and heart blown apart. Imagine the cruelty of opening up the womb of a pregnant woman, tearing the child out, and killing it in front of the bleeding mother. If they killed the mother, the baby would die. Why rip out the unborn baby and tear it to pieces in front of its mother? That is killing that mother mentally—killing her by shock first, before killing her physically. That is demonic.

The horror and the brutality were extreme in Rwanda. That's why when we talk about reconciliation, when we talk about forgiveness, we are not talking about an easy thing here. We are talking about shedding miles of tears before one is able to forgive. And to repent of such cruelty requires divine motivation and the divine presence just to attempt it. It cannot be done without God. As a human being, to be able to repent of such demonic cruelty requires the cross of Jesus right in the middle of it.

The reconciliation we are attempting here is not an easy thing. It is very painful. I have seen people try to talk about it and burst into tears for an hour or two before they can even speak.

The extremes during the Rwandan genocide have often been referred to as demonic. Even the killers can't explain their actions. "Now it seems to me that we were mad," a prisoner told me. "It was like a madness, a frenzy of killing. It was very exciting in a way because the authorities were there cheering you on, supporting you. But when I look back now, I see there was no reason for much of what we did. I killed babies with a machete, tiny babies. Why would I do that?" [18]

Some people were saved because the frenzy so overtook the killers that they ran about like madmen. They would hack at a person and then run off to kill someone else before finishing the job. Or they would be hacking away, and there would be a whistle calling them for a looting, and they would just leave the people they were killing and run off. Often they would forget to come back and finish.

One time a man was chopping at a young Tutsi man's head when he heard someone cough nearby. He dropped the machete and ran off, because he was afraid it was the RPF coming. So the Tutsi man ran and hid in a nearby school. He was a lecturer, and he hid in one of the lecturer's rooms. When the killers realized that the RPF had not come, they looked for him all over the school.

The man who had been attacking him told the others, "He was a tall man, so look for the tallest and kill him." So they searched the area and chose the tallest man they saw. He was a Hutu, but they killed him anyway. Just because he was tall! During the time they spent searching for this man, their anger grew to the point where they simply killed the tallest person they found.

In the last analysis, the primary agents of the genocide were ordinary peasants. The amount of force applied to get them to kill varied greatly from village to village, but in some cases the government's official story of a spontaneous movement to kill the Tutsi was true. This was the result of years of indoctrination that began with the Belgians. Although the peasants often had to be pushed into carrying out the massacres, once they began, the suppressed resentments sprang forth into a terrifying full-blown hatred.

A seventy-four-year-old man, captured by the RPF, said, "I regret what I did . . . but what would you have done if you'd been in my place? Either you took part in the massacre or else you were massacred yourself. So I took weapons and I defended my people against the Tutsi." [19]

Even as he expressed regret and claimed he was forced to do it, the man still described his actions as defensive. He admitted killing harmless people, and yet agreed with the dominating propaganda (which he now knows to be untrue) by describing the defenseless Tutsis as aggressive enemies.

As bizarre as it may sound, the Rwandan genocide is awash with "victim killers"—men, women, and children who often were horrified at what they had done and somewhat at a loss to explain it. "After the killing we started to feel bad when we heard on the radio about the genocide and how many had been killed," one man told me, "but when we killed, it was like we weren't ourselves. We didn't think about anything except the killing." [20]

Gitera, a Hutu farmer interviewed for the *Frontline* documentary, used similar terms to describe his participation in the killing of five thousand Tutsis at the church in Nyarubuye: "The leader told us that Tutsis had fled to Nyarubuye and that we're to go there and kill them. On the morning of April 15th, we woke up and started walking towards the church . . . It was as if we were taken over by Satan. When Satan is using you, you lose your mind. We were not ourselves. You couldn't be normal and you start butchering people for no reason." [21]

While many of the killers in Kigali were young, the killers in the villages were even younger. Children as young as ten years old were given machetes and told to do their duty, which sometimes meant murdering their former playmates. In one village the children were given the head of one of their Tutsi classmates to use as a soccer ball. Killing was often a family affair. Mothers with babies on their backs killed other mothers who also carried babies on their backs—with little hesitation or doubt that what they were doing might be wrong.

This is why the work of reconciliation is so desperate. Most of these people still live in the same villages. Only now there are new Tutsi families living there. Imagine the nightmares and confusion of a sixteen-year-old boy who remembers helping cut off the head of a classmate to use as a soccer ball when he was only five or six years old. Only God can heal such guilt.

There seems to be no end to the horrors of the Rwandan genocide. Although it was common knowledge that the goal was the elimination of every Tutsi in the country, it now seems ludicrous that such a thought was entertained, much less actually attempted. Indeed, some of the most horrific events grew out of the macabre idea that no Tutsi would be left to tell the story. Militiamen at the Kibungo diocese tracked down survivors emerging from a pile of eight hundred bodies. Then the men sifted through the corpses and systematically clubbed to death anyone who might have had the smallest flicker of life in his or her eyes.

Every atrocious way of killing was practiced. People were forced to watch their relatives burn alive. At Butare University, the Tutsi wife of a Hutu teacher was disemboweled in front of her husband, and the fetus of their unborn child was shoved in the man's face while the killers screamed, "Here! Eat your bastard!" A favorite trick of the killers was to try to force parents to kill their own children with the vain hope that the parents might then be spared.

Shaharyar Khan, the special representative of the secretary general of the United Nations wrote in his book, *The Shallow Graves of Rwanda:*

Never in living history has such wanton brutality been inflicted by human beings on their fellow creatures [as in Rwanda] . . . even the killing fields of Cambodia and Bosnia pale before the gruesome, awful, depravity of massacres in Rwanda . . . The Interahamwe made a habit of killing young Tutsi children, in front of their parents, by first cutting off one arm, then the other. They would then gash the neck with a machete to bleed the child slowly to death but, while they were still alive, they would cut off the private parts and throw them at the faces of the terrified parents, who would then be murdered with slightly greater dispatch.[22]

I know of a boy who was made to stand next to a wall that had nails driven through it so that the sharp ends were close to his flesh. They built a huge fire in front of him and grilled him alive. He couldn't go into the nails, and he couldn't go into the fire. He was saved just as the water in his body had dried up and parts of his flesh were beginning to fall off. Why take the time to plan out and do all that evil to a human being whom you don't know and who has never hurt you? There was such an evil presence in so much of this that we cannot cure it without God's presence. Our reconciliation has to engage God.

Some have theorized that the atrocities were throwbacks to the pagan religions of Africa, but even those primitive religions usually did not sacrifice human beings. They sacrificed animals and believed in evil taboos, but they had a code of conduct. You didn't kill a woman or a child. Only Satan worshipers did such things.

Rwanda's Misguided Faith

The satanic faith of Mobuto (the late president of the Congo) believed in sacrificing two hundred people after a season of time. They believed that the people should be killed in a way that satisfied the demon's thirst for blood. But the traditional beliefs of old Rwanda centered around being guided by right and hating evil. Our traditional beliefs maintained that evil people would go into the Nyamuragira, which is a volcanic mountain that is still active. It does not throw up lava, but burns at night.

The old beliefs of Rwanda were that all evil men would go into that burning, volcanic lava. Essentially, that is like believing in hell. It's the kind of belief that has God at the center, but without Jesus. I see that as the type of tolerated ignorance that Paul discussed in the Bible. It's a misguided faith that needs to be put right in Jesus Christ. But that cannot be compared with the satanic. The satanic is purely a rebellion against God. It is against right, against good. And it is designed in part to inflict pain on those who love God.

Satanism

The purpose of satanic worship is to try to gain earthly power. When Idi Amin was at his worst in Uganda, he was practicing satanic worship. He was bloodthirsty, and there were many rumors that he sacrificed human beings. There is even a rumor that he killed his son as a form of sacrifice to the demons. He killed his wife, Kay, the daughter of an Anglican clergyman.

Amin forced her into marriage after her university study and then, when he turned against religion and faith, dismembered her, cut her limb by limb and had the pieces put into a box. For a while Idi Amin claimed to be a Muslim, but he was never a good Muslim. He was more into Satanism.

The Genocide Planners and Satanism

Were the genocide planners into Satanism? They were certainly into power and had no trouble killing to obtain it, but there is no way to know if they envisioned the genocide as a blood sacrifice to the devil. What is more likely, however, is that the perpetrators of the genocide gave themselves over to the demonic more and more during the killing.

There is no question in my mind that anyone who kills his own wife or children is under demonic influence. There were many who did this without any enticement or intimidation. People killed their own children because they resembled their Tutsi mothers; people killed their nephews because they resembled their fathers who were Tutsi—even though the nephews were born of their sisters. People killed their sisters because they had married a Tutsi man.

People took babies and threw them against walls, or put them into frying pans and fried them. People took babies and put them in mortars and pounded the babies the way you would grind nuts or some other grain. No one can convince me that there was not demonic influence in all of this. And that convinces me even more to bring in the gospel, the teaching of our Lord Jesus Christ, to come against this demonic presence.

These were moments of demonic possession. That is why so many people cry out now and ask: "Why on earth did I do this? Why was I crazy to this extent?" Most people don't understand demonic possession. It's not like it is depicted in Hollywood movies, where a demon just jumps into a totally innocent person and possesses him. Those who have been possessed usually have made so many free-will choices for evil that the consequences of those choices have locked them into a path where they no longer have the power to choose otherwise. They have surrendered so much control to the devil that they no longer recognize the Holy Spirit and have lost the opportunity of having their consciences redeemed.

When a person steps out in the direction that Satan wants him or her to go, Satan empowers that step, it catches fire, and he or she goes farther in that direction. It doesn't matter if that person began by calling on the devil or not. He or she is doing his will and he will empower that and push it to a further extent. The prisoner at Ruhengiri explained it this way:

> When we were killing it felt like there was something pushing us from the inside, making us want to kill more and more. It was like a demon pushing us. It was as if the killing was not real sometimes. Other times it felt real, but it was like we had no choice or feeling, like a devil was forcing us. Sometimes I still can't believe we did it. I often dream about the killings. I know people who killed who have gone mad from remembering them.[23]

Interviews have confirmed that some of the villagers who killed moved from village to village as if in a trance, without even speaking. Other groups seemed to be in a constant rage, shouting and cursing for no reason, in a continual bloodlust. One thing that has been well researched is that people who participate in mass killings are able to block out any conscious analysis of what they are doing, but subconsciously they seem to be driven to darker and darker deeds. It is as though they are trying to prove something to themselves. It's as if the only way to snuff out the spark of guilt from yesterday's evil is to do something even worse today.

Each new horrible act seems to justify the previous acts. It is as if the mind is saying, *These people are not human, and therefore the evil that I did to them yesterday does not matter, and I will prove this by doing even worse things to them today.* So you have a continual worsening of actions moving further down the scale of evil. A man shoots someone he doesn't know the first day, then sets fire to a house in a distant village the second day, but by the fourth or fifth day he is killing his neighbor's children. Each new horrendous deed affirms to his diseased mind that the previous deeds were justifiable. Each new terrible deed to an even greater level denies the humanity of the people he is killing.

The killings in Rwanda included so many atrocities on such a mass scale that many who were there felt they had looked into the very heart of evil. General Dallaire, commander of the United Nations Mission in Rwanda, interviewed for the April 2004, PBS *Frontline* documentary entitled "The Ghosts of Rwanda," told how he finally convinced Bagosora to introduce him to the leaders of the Interahamwe: "As I was. . . . shaking their hands I noticed some blood spots on them. And all of a sudden . . . something happened that turned them into non-human things. I . . . was not talking with humans. I was . . . talking with evil. It . . . became a very difficult ethical problem. Do I actually negotiate with the devil to save people? Or do I wipe it out, shoot the bastards right there?"[24]

There is no denying the demonic aspects of the genocide in Rwanda. What is amazing is that so many people of faith allowed themselves to participate in it. Several government people who helped plan the genocide actually claimed to be churchgoing Catholics or Protestants, but they could not have done what they did and had any real belief in Jesus Christ. They were more like members of religious clubs than real Christians. They may have belonged to churches, but their beliefs were more like those of Satanists.

The Nazis

Most of the Nazis were registered members of three churches—Catholic, Lutheran, and Anglican—but it was in name only. They operated more like Satanists, and many of them had taken demonic oaths. Whatever motivated Hitler or the Rwandan community to killing, that inspiration, that urge, was not from God. That empowerment was not from the God I know and love and serve. It was demonic.

Involvement of the Clergy

Perhaps the most demonic aspect of the genocide in Rwanda was the involvement of so many clergy. The failure of the organized church is particularly tragic when one considers that before the genocide, Rwanda had often been called Africa's most Christian country, with 90 percent of the people identifying themselves as Christians (65 percent Roman Catholic and 25 percent other Christian faiths). Essentially that means people who dutifully attended church on Sunday were slaughtering their neighbors by the end of the week. How did people who supposedly followed Jesus pick up machetes and chop children to death?

While pastors and priests were by no means spared, and Tutsi and liberal Hutu priests were killed with their counterparts in the general population, the clergy as a whole did little to stop the slaughter. Even worse, there were pastors and priests who believed in the mission of the genocide and even helped kill people. I don't understand how a person could allow his ethnicity to transcend his faith, but the cold, dark truth is that most of the Hutu clergy simply looked the other way.

Some Clergy Were True to Their Faith

One should realize, however, that this became a matter of individual conscience—or lack or it. Just as there were pastors and priests who ignored their faith and killed, there were pastors and priests who lived out their faith and died. Some were Hutus, and some were Tutsis. There were Hutu pastors and priests who died trying to save their Tutsi congregations.

The head of the African Evangelistic Enterprise, Havugimana Israel, was killed. There were Hutu clergy who were not supposed to be killed, but were killed because they took a stand. A Hutu nun was killed because she would not leave the Tutsi Christians who had run to her for help. A Hutu pastor saved a Tutsi woman by hiding her and running with her until they escaped to the Congo. Even in the Congo they tried to kill him for helping her. He was prosecuted and put in jail for a time.

Historical Abuse

In the past the clergy often collaborated with colonial masters in their unfair practices, which sometimes included massacres. For example, in 1959 the

Catholic archbishop wrote a letter claiming that the Tutsis were communists, and any Christian who opposed them would receive indulgences from God.

When King Leopold gave up his rights to the Congo, the Belgium parliament refused to take on the budget for the colony because it was much bigger than the budget for Belgium. The Catholic Church offered to cofinance the colony to maintain control. After that, any political move Belgium wanted to make in the Congo had to be supported by the Church.

It was these kinds of abuses that caused much of Africa to embrace socialism and turn away from the churches. Unfortunately, the church didn't often stand for the welfare of the people. Even some of the church-sponsored educational programs were only to prepare the people to be better servants. They didn't teach how to think or create or plan or invent or to be who God meant us to be. Africans were only educated for better control.

Looking the Other Way and Active Participation

During the genocide the organized church reached a new low by more or less officially abandoning Rwandans to their fate, especially when they knew that meant certain death for so many. Although there were many admirable acts of courage by individual Christians, the church hierarchies were at best useless, and at worst accomplices in the genocide. Regrettably the church sided with the political regimes and did not denounce political and social injustice. It did not exercise its prophetic role and condemn the first mass killings, so by the time of the genocide, it was locked into looking the other way.

Some of the worst cases have led to prosecution. In September 2005, Father Guy Theunis, a member of the White Fathers congregation, was arrested at Kigali airport by Rwandan authorities as he prepared to board a plane to Brussels. Father Theunis, the former editor of a church-backed magazine, *Dialogue,* was accused of "crimes against humanity" for his involvement in the genocide. Father Athanase Seromba, the former priest in charge of the Nyange parish in Kibuye (western Rwanda), as of this writing is on trial for taking part in the genocide. Father Seromba allegedly ordered bulldozers to demolish his church while two thousand Tutsis were hiding inside.

In 2001, Sisters Maria Mukabutera and Gertrude Mukangango, two Rwandan Benedictine nuns, were found guilty of supplying the gasoline used to burn down a garage containing five hundred Tutsi refugees during the genocide. They were sentenced to twelve- and fifteen-year prison terms, respectively. Four days after the start of the genocide, several Catholic priests promised their "support to the new government." They asked all Rwandans to "respond favorably to calls" from the new authorities and to help them realize the goals they had set, including the return of peace and security. Unfortunately, one of these goals included killing a million people.

The late Anglican bishop, Samuel Musabyimana, was indicted because, on May 7, 1994, when soldiers and the militia arrived at Shyogwe diocese to transport Tutsi refugees to the killing sites, the bishop did not resist or use his influence with the interim government (which had held meetings in his house many times). He later fled Rwanda with the fallen government.

Pastor Elizaphan Ntakirutimana, a leading member of the Seventh-Day Adventist church in Rwanda, was found guilty in 2003 and sentenced to ten years in prison for his involvement in the genocide. The Seventh-Day Adventist's leadership apologized for the crimes committed by its pastors and stated that there had not been any church policy to support the genocide.

Although it can be said that Muslims did at least look out for their own, few, if any, of the organized faiths were exempt from wrongdoing in Rwanda. My church, the Angelican, has also apologized for the acts of some of its clergy. In regard to the Catholic Church, two years after the genocide, Pope John Paul II said, "The Church . . . cannot be held responsible for the guilt of its members who have acted against the law of the Gospel; they themselves will be called to give account of their actions . . . [Any Catholics guilty of war crimes are] to assume the consequences of the actions taken against God and against neighbor."[25]

While the Catholic Church denied any institutional blame, it paid legal fees for its clergy suspected of being involved in the genocide. The Church also aided fugitives and discouraged its members from cooperating with genocide tribunals. For the Catholic Church the extreme point of poor faith was

reached by twenty-nine priests who, on August 2, 1994, wrote a collective letter to the Pope in which they denied any Hutu responsibility for the genocide
and attributed it to the RPF, denouncing the idea of an international tribunal
to investigate crimes against humanity, and defending the FAR.

Catholic archbishop Augustin Nshamihigo and the assistant bishop of
Kigali, Jonathan Ruhumuliza, described the government responsible for
orchestrating the genocide as "peace-loving" at a Nairobi press conference in
early June 1994.

The accusations against other denominations are no less shocking. According
to survivors, Bishop Aaron Ruhumuliza, head of the Free Methodist Church in
Gikondo, Kigali, helped the militia carry out a massacre in his own church on
April 9, 1994. Michel Twagirayesu, the president of the Presbyterian Church of
Rwanda and a former vice president of the World Council of Churches, is alleged
to have worked closely with the killers in the Presbyterian stronghold of Kirinda,
Kibuye, betraying parishioners and fellow clergy alike, according to a report by
African Rights.

Racist Ideology

Unfortunately, the leadership of the Christian churches has long played a
central role in the furtherance of discriminatory ideology. The colonial masters introduced this ideology, but it was encouraged by many of the churches.
Church authorities spread theories through the schools and seminaries they
controlled, and most of the genocide planners were educated in these schools.

Church leaders should have taken a stance against discrimination, instead of
convincing people to accept a morally reprehensible policy and condemning
those who spoke out against it. Before and after the genocide, influential clergymen spread the stereotypes used to dehumanize Tutsis. The racist political party
Parmehutu was, in fact, organized by Belgium and the Catholic Church.

Individual clergy have not always agreed with such policies. The racially
motivated quota system introduced by the Rwandan government was fully
supported by the Catholic Church, but on April 30, 1990, five Catholic priests
from the Nyundo diocese wrote a letter to the Church's bishops in Rwanda,

calling the quota system "racist" and urged that it was high time "the Church of Jesus Christ established in Rwanda proclaimed aloud and tirelessly" to denounce it, since it constituted "an aberration" within their Church. They maintained that the only sure justice in schools and employment only took account of individual capacities, regardless of people's origins and that it was on this condition that the country could have citizens capable of leading it with competence and equity.[26]

The letter ended: "The Church should not be the vassal of the secular powers, but it should be free to speak with sincerity and courage when it proves necessary."[27] The authors of this brave letter were Father Augustin Ntagara, Father Callixte Kalisa, Father Aloys Nzaramba, Father Jean Baptiste Hategeka, and Father Fabien Rwakareke. All but the last two were killed during the genocide.

Many people in Rwanda have realized that the failure of church leaders is a tragedy, but one that has little to do with God. God is above such injustice, and God certainly did not approve of it. Our hope in the promises of God is that when we call on His name in truth and with a sincere heart, He will heal us and restore our nation. We clergy need to be honest with God and seek His forgiveness in repentance. Then we can ask for the release of His empowerment to preach true reconciliation in Rwanda.

Heroes

There were innumerable heroes during the Rwandan genocide. No list would be complete that failed to mention at least a few. In the memorial at Kigali, a few stories are told.

Gahiga Nsengiyumva was a Muslim living in Nyamirambo. During the genocide he is reported to have saved the lives of more than thirty people whom he protected or hid in his outhouse. One of the people he saved told this story: "The Interahamwe killers were chasing me down the alley. I was going to die any second. I banged on the door of the yard. It opened almost immediately. He [Nsengiyumva] took me by the hand and stood in the doorway and told the killers to leave. He said the Koran said, "If you save one life it is like saving the whole world." He did not know it was a Jewish text as well." [28]

Sulyi Karembi was a seventy-year-old widow when she hid seventeen Tutsis in a shelter she had made for animals. She used her reputation as a woman possessed by evil spirits to scare the Interahamwe away from her home. She told them that if they entered the shrine, they would incur the wrath of the Nyabigyi. This frightened them away.

Kamujay Frodward saved the lives of fourteen Tutsis in Gitarama, protecting them for more than a month. He hid refugees in trenches that he dug on his land. His sister cooked, and his twelve-year-old niece took the food disguised in a dustbin to the hidden Tutsis. Frodward put plants and green banana leaves over the Tutsis' hiding place. Then he piled earth on top of this and planted seed potatoes all along the top of the trench.

Thamaze Kazingery Gasamba took into his orphanage at Nyamirambo about four hundred orphans, refugees, and employees from April to June 1994. He even rescued some people who had been thrown into the mass graves. With the help of the International Red Cross and Adventist Development, a relief agency, Thamaze was able to evacuate the majority to St. Michel Cathedral.

We do not even know the last names of Sefa and Odette. Odette was on the run in Kigali during the genocide when someone told her to go to Sefa's house for safety. She arrived late at night. On answering the door Sefa said, "I've been expecting you all day, but so many people have arrived since I heard you were coming that there is no longer any space in my house where you can hide." But when Odette walked away weeping, Sefa called to her, "Come back or your tears will judge me forever." Sefa hid Odette with many others fleeing the killing. She brought home wounded people found among the corpses and tended their wounds. So many came to her house that she placed blocks on the legs of her bed so that more could hide beneath it.

Jean-Marie Vianey De Solara was the *bourgmestre* of Nyabisindu. He refused to support Hutu extremist ideology, so when the militia attacked Decongera, he used the Comonet police force to defeat the Interahamwe. Jean-Marie was killed along with eleven members of his family. He was the only person in authority in Nadasimba who discouraged people from hurting one another. He gave his life in the course of peace.

Many of these unsung heroes were Christians, whose love and courage made up in some way for the compromises of their church. Hutu Catholic lay worker Felicite Niyitegeka is not mentioned at the Kigali memorial, but she helped a great many people cross the border near Gisenyi. Her brother, an army colonel, wrote to tell her that the militia knew of her activity, but she refused to stop. When they finally came to get her, she had thirty refugees in her house.

The Interahamwe said she would be spared, but her charges would have to be killed. She answered that they would all stay together, in life or in death. To make her recant, the militiamen then shot the refugees one by one before her eyes. When the slaughter was over, she asked to be killed. The militia leader asked her to pray for his soul before shooting her. In times as fraught with evil as the Rwandan genocide, even basic kindness could lead to death. Such is the story of the Hutu family who could no longer bear the sight of the naked body of their Tutsi neighbor and covered it with some banana leaves. For this simple act of humanity, the Interahamwe killed all of them.

The RPF on the Move

From the time that the RPF renewed fighting, they made much headway. Gabiro had fallen, and the rebel army now held the entire Ugandan–Rwandan border in the east. Kagame avoided attacking the capital until the French left, to prevent giving them any provocation to intervene. Instead he moved to corner the RGF in Byumba and seized the Tanzanian border to close in on Kigali from the east.

In retrospect, General Kagame proved to be one of the truly great strategists of maneuver warfare in modern military history. The downside to his maneuvering was that it took time, and thousands of Tutsis were dying daily at that time. In another sense, Kagame knew that the ultimate survival of Tutsis in Rwanda depended upon him winning the war. If he had not stopped his assault in favor of the Arusha Peace Accords, he might have taken the capital before the genocide was launched.

Kigali Memorial where over 250,000 are
buried in mass graves

Skulls on display at Kigali Memorial

Corpses preserved in limestone at Murambi
Center where 40–50,000 were murdered

Belongings found in genocide victims' clothing

Inside church at Ntarama where 5,000 Rwandans lost their lives

Ibuka (Remember) genocide memorial crosses

Prisoners returning to prison after a work day; uniforms are pink.

St. John's Cathedral

Full-house services at St. John's Cathedral

Local public school near St. John's Cathedral

Sonrise High School

Shyira Diocese high school
drum and dance team

Children who will benefit from coffee
cooperative in Shyira Diocese

A regular meeting providing HIV/AIDS
education in the Shyira Diocese

Sonrise Primary School, Shyira Diocese

Students in class at Sonrise Primary School

Sonrise Primary School children singing in French and English

Sonrise Primary School boys enjoying recess

End of school day fun at Sonrise Primary School

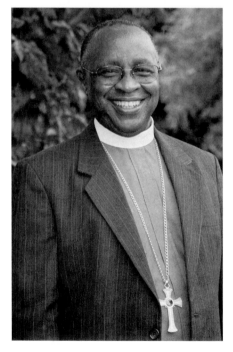

Bishop John Rucyahana and Harriet Rucyahana

Bishop John Rucyahana

Bishop Rucyahana teaching
after Sunday services

Bishop John and Harriet Rucyahana with
youth choir

Children leaving services to go to Sunday
school

Sunday services recessional

Sorghum harvest

Common daily life in Rwanda

Gakenke, a typical small town in northern
Rwanda

Children at play

He no longer trusted anything that came out of Kigali. He knew the government would do anything to hold on to power and eliminate the Tutsi—even kill its own president. He did not trust the UN, because he did not trust the international community that controlled them. The Hutu extremists had counted on the fact that the international community would do nothing to stop the genocide, and they were right. They also counted on their ability to brainwash the peasants through fear and the manipulation of their natural loyalty—and they had been right on that as well. Finally, they counted on their capacity to resist the RPF military. Knowing the future of Rwanda was in his hands, Kagame was determined to prove them wrong.

Kigali

Six weeks into the genocide, Kigali had turned into something akin to the last reel of a zombie movie or a futuristic no man's land, where evil reigned, guns ruled, and fear dominated every breath. There were roadblocks all over the city and piles of bodies at each one. Every so often, trucks came and hauled the bodies away, but a new pile soon began growing in its place. At each checkpoint lines of people waited to have their identity cards checked.

What is so amazing is how many of those people simply stood in line waiting to die. Tutsis were killed on the spot. In some places, a Hutu could buy passage for his Tutsi wife, but in others the Interahamwe would order him to kill her right in front of them. There were still pockets of Tutsis hiding all over the city. Sometimes neighbors or people who wanted their jobs or property would turn them in.

Occasionally, one heard of a kindhearted GP soldier or Interahamwe who, for some unknown reason, would look the other way when moments before he might have killed someone he had known his entire life. There were no rules. Most men created their own moral standard for the time.

For example, Father Wenceslas Munyashyaka, the curate of Sainte-Famille church in Kigali, sheltered eight thousand refugees, but also agreed to let the militia pick off those they wanted every now and then. He provided safety for several thousands of people, but freely agreed to turn over others from the lists of names that were brought to him.

Carl Wilkens, an aid worker with the Adventist Church, was one of the last white men in Kigali. He stayed behind to provide a hiding place for some Tutsis and hadn't left his apartment for weeks. When he did, he was startled to find a different Kigali.

> It was weird. There were horses roaming the streets, and there are no horses in Rwanda except at the Belgian club. Someone . . . must have let them out of their stalls. There were guys sitting at roadblocks in couches, and they'd have an old shotgun across their lap and they'd have like a monkey on a leash— some foreigner's pet who'd fled. Little kids were playing with . . . Western toys . . . Little Rwandan kids had never seen these toys before, much less been able to . . . play with them.[29]

A few days later, Wilkens was out driving when he came across an orphan-age surrounded by fifty armed men. Realizing there must be Tutsi children inside, he decided to visit the government offices and see what he could do.

> I went to the headquarters office and a young secretary I'd become friends with . . . [told me] the colonel wasn't in; he was out of town that day, but his assis-tant [was] eating down in the basement. So I said, "Well, I'll go to Mark at the other orhanage two blocks away, and I'll be right back" [When he] got back, he said, "He's down [there], but you won't believe it—the prime minister's here." I'm like, "So what's that mean?" and he's like, "Ask him."
>
> I'm like, "Ask him?" It's like that's the stupedist thing you could imagine— to ask this guy who is obviouly orchestrating the genocide, a key player, and yet I have no other options . . . [He's like], "Just go out in the hallway. He's in the next office. When he comes out, ask him." So I went out [into the hallway] . . . and [a] door opens. Everybody snaps to attention, and here comes [the prime minister] and his little entourage. They're coming down the hall, and I am, too.
>
> I put my hand out and I said, "Mr. Prime Minister, I'm Carl Wilkins, the

director of ADRA." He stops and he looks at me, and then he takes my hand and shakes it and said, "Yes, I've heard about you and your work. How is it?" I said, "Well, honestly, sir, it's not very good right now. The orphans at Gisimba are surrounded, and I think there's going to be a massacre, if there hasn't been already." He turns around, talks to some of his aides or whatever, [and he turns back to me and] he says, "We're aware of the situation, and those orphans are going to be safe. I'll see to it."[30]

The orphans were saved. By having the courage to face evil, good was accomplished. General Dallaire had a similar situation when he again met with the Interahamwe leaders in May.

This time as I was removing my pistol, which was the etiquette for such meetings, I hesitated, certainly long enough to be noticed, then let my gun drop on the sofa. I don't know what the three Interahamwe leaders made of the gesture, but I was fighting a terrible compulsion to shoot them on the spot. This was no fleeting urge. I had to consciously take my weapon off and put it away from myself. Why not shoot them? Wouldn't such an act be justified? They spoke their words of welcome, and I let the chance go. I still debate the choices of that moment in my head. [This time the Interahamwe leaders were neatly dressed without any blood spots.]

The three riders of the apocalypse were all smiling at me, apparently proud of the fact that I had come to see them again . . . I said that I wanted to operate with all forces in Rwanda, including them. I told them that UNAMIR 2 would be a humanitarian-focused mission, not an intervention force. Kajunga assured me again of the movement's cooperation. The Interahamwe pledged to work diligently for the halt of the massacres and the return to peace.[31]

Why not? They had already run out of Tutsis to kill.

Life in Kigali near the end of May was a constant threat. On the last day of the month, Captain Diange Mbaye was making a run from the Hotel des Mille Collines to the UNAMIR base of operations when he came to a checkpoint on the bridge. While he waited behind a few cars, a mortar shell hit behind his vehicle, sending shrapnel into the car. He was dead before he hit the dashboard. Mbaye had saved the lives of Prime Minister Agathe's children and probably hundreds more. He had braved direct and indirect fire, mines, mobs, disease, and more, picking up refugees and hiding them until he could find safety for them. He was a hero in every sense of the word.

Gromo Alex, a veteran UN aid worker, helped prepare Mbaye's body for shipment back to Senegal. "Here's a guy who gave his ultimate . . . and we don't even have a body bag to show him some respect . . . We had some UNICEF plastic sheeting, and we had some tape . . . you wanted it [perfect for him] so that when people look at him, they know that he was something great."[32]

There was little media coverage about Mbaye's death, not like there would have been if he'd been British or American. He was just another dead African. Another hero in a gulf of evil that was swallowing Africans by the thousands.

Lack of Response from the International Community

There is no question that the international community failed Rwanda. There are many reasons why the superpowers and the UN refused to get involved in stopping the genocide, and most of them are political. The few that are not are based around profit or the lack of profit. The risk was high, and the rewards were low. Rwanda didn't have anything that the superpowers cared about. No oil, no natural gas deposits, no gold, and not much of anything else. All Rwanda had was people.

As early as April 7, President Clinton issued a statement that the U.S. was "shocked and deeply saddened . . . horrified that elements of the Rwandan security forces have sought out and murdered Rwandan officials . . . extend my condolences . . . condemn these actions and I call on all parties to cease any such actions immediately—"[33]

For the first few days after President Habyarimana's plane was shot down, the international community was unsure what was happening in Rwanda. Within forty-eight hours the intelligence gathering services of the United States and the other major powerful nations had a pretty fair idea of the situation. Most of them claimed ignorance, because they didn't want to get involved. "They cannot tell . . . me that they didn't know," Philippe Gaillard of the International Red Cross maintained . . . They were told every day. Everyone knew."[34]

General Dallaire agreed:

Certainly France, the United Kingdom, China, Russia and the United States, the permanent five of the Security Council, all had fully equipped and manned embassies in Rwanda, including both military and intelligence attaches. None of the means of communications used in Rwanda by the political or military hierarchies had encryption capabilities, except for a few communications assets within the RPF. Between human and signal intelligence on the ground and worldwide space- and air-based surveillance systems, these nations either knew in detail what was going on or they were totally asleep at the switch. I firmly doubt they were asleep. The French, the Belgians, and the Germans had military advisers numbering in the dozens at all levels of the military and gendarme command and training structures in Rwanda.[35]

Uninformed?

Dallaire's suspicions were somewhat confirmed when he was warned indirectly by U.S. intelligence of a plan to assassinate him. "I guess I should have been grateful for the tip, but my larger reaction was that if delicate intelligence like this could be gathered by surveillance, how could the United States not be recording evidence of the genocide occurring in Rwanda?"[36]

The UN certainly knew, because Dallaire had been telling them it was going to happen, and now he was telling them that it was happening. And the UN, more than anyone else, had a responsibility to act, an official and designated responsibility to act—one they chose to ignore.

The Power in a Word

On December 11, 1946, the General Assembly of the United States declared genocide a crime under international law. On December 9, 1948, the General Assembly went even further, adopting Resolution 260A(III), the Convention on the Prevention and Punishment of the Crime of Genocide, which obliged "Contracting Parties" to "undertake to prevent and to punish . . . acts committed with intent to destroy, in whole or in part, a national, ethnical, racial or religious group.[37]

Instead of rushing in troops to stop the genocide, the United Nations spent weeks avoiding the issue. For example, on April 30, 1994, the UN Security Council spent eight hours discussing the Rwandan crisis. They issued a resolution condemning the killing, but it carefully omitted the word *genocide*. They simply avoided using the term so they would not have to honor the above resolutions. If the term *genocide* had been used, the UN would have been legally obliged to act to "prevent and punish" the "perpetrators." What makes all of this even worse is that Bagosora and the others who planned the genocide knew that the UN would react this way.

They had done their homework.

In Washington, D.C., the avoidance of the word *genocide* by politicians and their staffs became ludicrous. On April 28, state department spokesperson Christine Shelley was asked if what was happening in Rwanda was a genocide. She responded as follows: "The use of the term "genocide" has a very precise legal meaning, although it's not strictly a legal determination. There are other factors in there as well."[38]

On May 25, State Department spokesman Mike McCurry, was asked at a press briefing if the administration had yet come to any decision on whether the situation in Rwanda could be described as genocide. He answered, "I'll have to confess, I don't know the answer to that. I know that the issue was under very active consideration. I think there was a strong disposition within the department here to view what has happened there; certainly, constituting acts of genocide that have occurred."[39]

On June 10, at a State Department briefing, after also referring to "acts of genocide," Christine Shelley was asked, "How many acts of genocide does it take to make genocide?"

She replied, "That's just not a question that I'm in a position to answer."[40]

A reporter then asked, "Well, is it true that you have specific guidance not to use the word 'genocide' in isolation, but always to preface it with these words 'acts of'?" Shelly answered:

I have guidance which I try to use as best as I can. There are formulations that we are using that we are trying to be consistent in our use of. I don't have an absolute categorical prescription against something, but I have the definitions. I have phraseology which has been carefully examined and arrived at as best as we can apply to exactly the situation and the actions which have taken place.[41]

When pressed further, Shelley tried to explain the situation by saying, "Although there have been acts of genocide in Rwanda, all the murders cannot be put into that category."[42]

This logic would excuse Hitler, since he committed a great many other killings besides the genocide against the Jews.

Besides the reports they were getting from Dallaire, the UN sent a special delegation to Rwanda to investigate human rights, and they found that genocide was in progress. By the end of April, a secret intelligence report by the U.S. State Department had been issued calling the killings a genocide. But neither report advised intervention. The UN delegation reported that the only reason to intervene would be to save human life. And that just wasn't enough.

The Role of the United States

When one reviews the UN's policy meetings on Rwanda at this time, it is the United States that seemed to be the chief obstacle to helping Rwanda. On May 13, 1994, the Security Council prepared to vote on whether or not to honor Dallaire's request to restore UNAMIR's strength in Rwanda. United

States representative Madeleine Albright delayed the vote for four days.[43] On May 17, the UN agreed to send sixty-eight hundred troops and policemen to Rwanda with the power to defend civilians.

A Security Council resolution said: "Acts of genocide may have been committed," but the sending of the mainly African UN forces was delayed because of arguments led by the United States over who would pay the bill and provide the equipment.[44] This debate slowed things down for more than a month. Gen. Roméo Dallaire described what finally happened.

I had judged that we needed one hundred APCs [armored personnel carriers] to be effective on the ground. The DPKO [UN department of peacekeeping organizations] approached fifty-four nations to give, lend or lease APCs to the troop-contributing African countries to equip their forces. The United States, with its vast unused Cold War stocks of APCs, eventually supplied fifty . . . then the stalling began: staff with the Pentagon were reluctant to put their vehicles into central Africa . . .

Then the United States decided that the APCs could not be given to the mission but would have to be leased and that the lease would have to be negotiated. Eventually they came up with the price of $4 million, which they insisted had to be prepaid. When the issue was raised of transporting the carriers to Kampala to link them up with the Ghanaians who needed to be trained to operate them, the United States insisted upon another $6 million to cover the cost of air transport . . . after much negotiation with Uganda, they arrived stripped of machine guns, radios, tools, spare parts, training manuals, and so on. The United States, in effect, delivered tons of rusting metal to Entebbe. We were without trucks to transport the APC5 to Kigali and had no drivers trained to operate them.[45]

There was little help from other nations. The British offered fifty Bedford trucks, also requiring a sizable amount of money to be paid up front. "The Bedford is an early Cold War–era truck," Dallaire said, "which in 1994 was fit only to be a museum relic."[46]

The British later withdrew their request for payment and provided some of the vehicles that the UNAMIR used until they broke down, one at a time.

In addition to Rwanda's lack of natural resources, there were other reasons the international community responded so poorly to Rwanda's need. General Dallaire later became familiar with some of them:

> Rwanda was on nobody's radar as a place of strategic interest. It had no natural resources and no geographical significance. It was already dependent on foreign aid just to sustain itself, and on international funding to avoid bankruptcy. Even if the mission were to succeed . . . there would be no political gain for the contributing nations; the only real beneficiary internationally would be the UN . . . Member nations do not want a large, strong, and independent United Nations . . . What they want is a weak, beholden, indebted scapegoat of an organization, which they can blame for their failures or steal victories from.[47]

The United States generally spearheads most humanitarian moves that the UN makes, but they provided more resistance than assistance over the idea of intervening in Rwanda. Most experts agree that this was because the U.S. lost both lives and credibility in Somalia during the summer of 1993. As a result, the United States wanted to avoid any possible entanglement in Rwanda.

The Role of the UN

There is another, simpler explanation as to why the UN, which had the knowledge, the power, and the mandate, did not stop the genocide. First, let us ask: Who controls the United Nations? The members of the Security Council are France, Britain, Germany, the United States, Russia, and China—most of whom are former colonizers of Africa. France was the acting head of the Security Council during the time of the genocide, and France was heavily involved in the genocide. Their soldiers trained the killing squads, they fought with the government against the RPF, and they paid for the machetes that the government ordered for use in the genocide.

France didn't want the genocide stopped. They were part of it. After all, Hutu Power—genocidal or not—presented no threat to European interests. Who remembers the half million Chinese killed on the orders of President Suharto of Indonesia in 1965? Or those massacred in Armenia or Cambodia, or those being killed right now in the Sudan? There was no way that France, the acting head of the Security Council, was going to send in UN troops to stop something they had trained people and supplied weapons to accomplish.

Rwanda must unite together! The only way there can be lasting peace in Rwanda is for Rwandans to unite and turn to God and not depend upon the superpowers. Only then will we find peace.

SEVEN

Bodies in the River

Operation Turquoise

By the end of June, the RPF had the government forces on the run in most places, and the world was starting to hear about the genocide in Rwanda. For these reasons the French decided to launch Operation Turquoise. While proclaimed as a rescue operation for Rwanda, Operation Turquoise was designed to rescue defeated government soldiers, Interahamwe, and Hutu peasants who had participated in the genocide. The French were coming to save their former allies, who were now fleeing from the RPF. They were not coming to save the people for humanitarian reasons, as they implied to the rest of the world. France was coming to rescue their friends.

Enormous French Tricolors were displayed everywhere, even on RGF military vehicles. Operation Turquoise gave the former government people and the Interahamwe time to make arrangements with Zaire (the Congo). The French escorted their allies to Zaire and established refugee camps in the hope that they could regroup and return to fight. It is against UN policy to rescue armed military personnel and let them take their weapons, their tanks, and hardware into camps like this. But France and the UN let that happen.

Only a few weeks before, on June 21, the *Liberation,* the same French newspaper that had published Foreign Minister Alain Juppe's call to arms a few days before, published an article called "Rwanda—a Death Squad Veteran Accuses," in which a former death-squad (Zero Network) member said he had been trained by French instructors. A week earlier, Colonel Dominique Bon, an attaché at the French embassy in Kinshasa, admitted that weapons were still being delivered to the RGP. Shortly after this information was released, Amnesty International issued a communiqué asking the French government to clarify its past involvement with the Rwandan death squads. The French delayed replying for some time, but eventually denied the report.

In early July, French soldiers created what was called the Zone Turquoise in the southwestern part of the country, proclaiming it a neutral zone, but that really meant that former government officials, the Interahamwe, and what was left of the RGF army could hide from the RPF there. The RGF still controlled the northwestern part of Rwanda, but the RPF controlled all the rest.

The French, though they brought all kinds of weapons, brought very few trucks or any kind of vehicle suited to a rescue operation. When the Tutsis saw the French soldiers, they came out of hiding, and the French would tell them to wait while they left to secure transportation. Then, while they were in the open, the Interahamwe came and slaughtered them. When the French returned, there would be only corpses. This happened at Bisesero, where hundreds of Tutsis died. There were many cases in which people that came for help during Operation Turquoise, were handed over to the Interahamwe and killed.

French soldiers, who had long been told that the trouble in Rwanda was only a civil war, were stunned. The French media began to broadcast interviews with soldiers who were shocked that it was their allies who were responsible for the massacres, and not the RPF, as they had been told by their superiors. The French troops, who had been given a slanted view of events, "were rudely awakened when they began to realise the relationship France had entertained with the Rwandese authorities. As a French soldier protested, 'I am fed up with being cheered along by murderers.'"[1]

It is no coincidence that the genocide reached near perfection in the area controlled the longest by the government troops and, unfortunately, in parts of Zone Turquoise as well. In the language of the Hutu extremists, these areas were "properly cleansed." There were very few survivors from the Kibuye area, for example.

The Last Days of Kigali

The capital city was now immersed in the effects of the genocide. It was besieged with disease, especially malaria, the result of having thousands of bodies in the streets for so long. Life was almost unbearable. Disease-ridden rats and corpse-eating dogs roamed the streets, with no qualms about attacking the living. There were still killings going on in the city, but they now had a desperate quality about them, as if the killers knew their days were numbered. At St. Paul's Church, Tutsi children were protected throughout the genocide, but suddenly on June 14, the Interahamwe entered the church and grabbed about forty children and killed them on the street.

Many Tutsis, who had been hiding since the outbreak of the genocide, were now emerging and trying to escape to the RPF, which was now as close as the airport. Committed to the last and made anxious by the closing in of the RPF, the Interahamwe and what was left of the Presidential Guard were now pretending to be RPF in order to lure people out of hiding so they could kill them.

Hearing of these atrocities inspired the RPF troops to new levels of daring. Six hundred Tutsis had been holed up in the Sainte Famille church in east Kigali since early April. Fearing they would be killed, the RPF sent a company of men over two miles inside enemy territory and rescued them, taking them to safety back through the RGF lines. The mission ended in a running battle with carefully planned artillery support. It was during this effort to save the people at Saint Famille that my nephew, Lieutenant Emmanuel, lost his life as he fell behind while carrying an old woman.

Interestingly enough, for those who celebrate freedom, it was at dawn on July 4 that the government forces withdrew from Kigali and gave the capital over to the RPF. Whether they had been outfought or just outlasted is not clear, but the answer is probably both. General Dallaire said from the evidence he found in and around the government's defensive positions, it looked as if they had run out of ammunition. In any case, Kigali was now under the control of the RPF. Even the Interahamwe was nowhere to be seen. But then again, there were no Tutsis left alive in the capital for them to kill.

On July 12, Philippe Gaillard, the head of the International Committee of the Red Cross, announced that a million people had been killed in the genocide. Though most of the press stayed with the eight hundred thousand, Gaillard's estimate was closer to the truth. As of this writing we have found and buried 1,117,000 bodies from the hundred days of the genocide.

On July 13, the RPF captured Ruhengeri, near the former home base of President Habyarimana and where my church is located today. The government forces had nowhere to run in Rwanda except into the arms of the French. On the sixteenth, Bagosora and most of his cabinet did just that, fleeing into the Zone Turquoise. France had promised to arrest them, but on July 17, Colonel Bagosora and his entourage moved on to Zaire. On the same day, Gen. Paul Kagame announced that he would form a new government in Kigali that would be guided by the power-sharing principles of the Arusha Accords and without regard to ethnicity.

The changing events elicited a response from the White House. On July 15, a "Statement by the press secretary on Rwanda" was released, which announced: "The Clinton Administration has closed the Embassy of Rwanda and ordered all personnel to leave the country. Representatives of the so-called interim government of Rwanda must depart within five working days."[2] The release also stated:

[The Clinton administration would] begin consultations with other United Nations Security Council members to remove representatives of the interim government from Rwanda's seat on the council . . . [and that the U.S. has] denied access to any Rwandan government financial holdings in the United States. "The United States cannot allow representatives of a regime that supports genocidal massacre to remain on our soil," President Clinton said.

[The U.S.] has taken a leading role in efforts to protect the Rwandan people and ensure humanitarian assistance. It has:

Provided more than $95 million in relief . . .

Flown about 100 Defense Department missions . . .

Strongly supported and expanded UNAMIR; airlifted 50 armored personnel carriers to Kampala . . . [and is} equipping the U.N.'s Ghanaian peacekeeping battalion.[3]

General Dallaire was surprised: "Clinton's fibbing dumbfounded me. The DPKO was still fighting with the Pentagon for military cargo planes to move materiel. The Pentagon had actually refused to equip the Ghanaians as they felt the bill was too high and that Ghana was trying to gouge them. And who exactly got the $95 million?"[4]

The Hutu Exodus

As the RPF gained ground, more and more Hutus left the country through most of June. For months the government and Radio RTLMC had told them that the RPF soldiers would massacre them on sight, and now they fled the approaching army. Many of these people had done no wrong, but among them were government organizers, the Interahamwe killers, and the worst of the Hutu peasants, who had massacred thousands upon thousands of innocent people.

The exodus from Rwanda turned into a human torrent of incredible proportions. At its peak, more than a million people walked along a sixty-kilometer stretch of road. It was a man swarm. All along the path were the sick and wounded—collapsed and receiving no help. Children were abandoned along the route by the thousands, lost in the shuffle and often deliberately left behind. Perhaps their parents believed they were better off, or perhaps it was because the parents could move more swiftly without them. The people were so overwrought with fear and anger, trauma and hopelessness, that either was possible.

It was a bizarre sight. There were priests leading their entire congregations along the road, and businessmen driving their cars loaded with material possessions right behind them. Entire family groups—parents, children, grandparents, uncles, aunts, and cousins walked together. Army battalions rolled through the crowd, and gunfire erupted periodically, usually triggering a stampede; people were crushed to death by the dozens.

All along the route RGF soldiers shot guns in the air to urge the people on. The Gisenyi prefect sent cars equipped with loudspeakers to further stampede the crowd toward the Zaire border, but most people needed little urging beyond the rumble of RPF artillery that could be heard in the distance. Indeed, the RPF trailed the mob into the northwest, the home of Hutu Power, seizing control of the country as they went.

The Refugee Camps

Another bizarre aspect of the genocide in Rwanda was what was allowed to happen in the refugee camps in the bordering countries. In a matter of days, millions of refugees had spilled over the border into Zaire, the Congo, Burundi, and Tanzania. A million crossed into Zaire in less than a week, and a half million trudged across the bridge at Rusumo to enter Tanzania. It was the largest dislocation of a population ever witnessed by the UNHCR (United Nations High Commissioner for Refugees).

The governments of the countries that bordered Rwanda, fearful that the influx of people would destabilize their systems, worked with the UN to establish refugee camps in each of their nations. Though no one can claim to have accurate figures, the best estimates are that 850,000 people settled in the six Zaire camps at Goma, 332,000 at Bukavu, and 62,000 at Uvira, making a total of 1,244,000 in Zaire alone. In addition, 577,000 went to camps in western Tanzania, 270,000 to those in northern Burundi, and 10,000 to the camp in southwestern Uganda. The UNHCR total figure of 2.1 million was later disputed by the United States Committee for Refugees, who put the figure at 1.7 million, but the distribution ratios are about the same.

Another Version of Hell

The camps were the largest refugee camps in history for such a short time from one nation. The sheer numbers in the camps that required food, clothing, and medical care doomed them to failure, and the camps quickly became another version of hell. In Zaire, the masses lacked everything—food, medicine, shelter, and clean water. This last item, when combined with the fact that there was also a serious shortage of latrines, because it was extremely hard to dig into the volcanic lava ground, soon led to an outbreak of cholera.

In addition to the unsanitary conditions, the camps were made up of people who had been exposed to thousands of dead bodies for more than two months. There was soon a full-fledged epidemic, which mushroomed because of overcrowding. By the end of the first week, there were six hundred deaths a day. By the end of the second week, there were three thousand deaths a day. The French soldiers attached to the rear echelon of the Turquoise "rescue" operation in Goma, soon became mass-grave diggers out of necessity.

"We Have the Population!"

As if this wasn't bad enough, the camps were also doomed by the autonomy that they were given. The same people who were in charge in the Rwanda government and the Interahamwe killing squads took charge of the camps. Consequently, any Tutsis found in the camps were quickly killed. In Tanzania, Remy Gatete, the prefect of Kibungo, took control of the entire camp and immediately announced that anyone who talked to journalists or human rights activists about what had happened in Rwanda would be killed.

In a move that became common to all of the camps, Gatete decreed that no one was to go back to Rwanda. The perpetrators of the genocide had masterminded the exodus, at least in part. And though they may have lost militarily to the RPF, they were a long way from surrendering. As former CDR leader Jean-Bosco Barayagwiza stated at the time: "Even if the RPF has won a military victory, it will not have the power. It has only the bullets; we have the population." And they intended on keeping them. The thinking among the former government members was that if Rwanda remained with a large area virtually unpopulated, the French could present an argument to the United Nations that you can't have a government without people, and they might be allowed to return to power with the population. It was a pretty ludicrous thought, but then so was killing every Tutsi in the country.

At the Zaire camp, Gatete was reputed to execute anyone who tried to go home. With the blanket condemnation of Tutsis and any Hutus who sympathized with them, the gag order on talking to officials, and the threats to those talking about leaving, the result was that there were murders every night in the camps. The living hell that had been life in Rwanda from April to June was now being continued in the camps.

As early as July 20, the former government's RGF forces and the Interahamwe began raiding emergency shipments of relief food and supplies that had been airlifted to Tanzania for the refugees. Before long, Gatete began siphoning off humanitarian aid to support his thugs in camp, and this soon also became the case in most of the other camps. The former leaders not only monopolized the distribution of humanitarian aid, but they also inflated the numbers of people actually registered, in order to receive more than was needed. As far as distribution of the aid, however, they gave first priority to themselves, and then to former government troops and the Interahamwe. What was left over was sold to obtain cash for the financing of future political or military operations.

The Tanzanian government was reluctant to use force to break up the power structure, and it was difficult to find people who would testify as to what was happening. UNHCR (the UN refugee relief organization), the Red Cross, and others trying to help had no power when it came to ousting the political cadres in control in the camps. And as it was during the genocide, the passivity of the population allowed the people in power to literally get away with murder. Once again, Rwanda's culture of obedience worked against its people.

Seeing no alternative, the aid agencies continued to do what they could, which was provide aid, and ironically, this reinforced the abuse. The Zaire camps were costing their sponsors at least a million dollars a day. This may not sound like much for a million people, especially when at least 70 percent of that money had to go for overhead—supplies, equipment, staff housing, salaries, benefits, and other assorted expenses for the aid workers, but the truth is that even twenty-five cents a day for each refugee was nearly twice the per capita income of most Rwandans.

In a study conducted by the World Bank after the genocide, Rwanda had become the poorest country on earth, with an average income of eighty dollars a year and probably 95 percent of the population was living on an average income closer to sixty dollars a year, or sixteen cents a day. On July 21, the United States committed to sending $76 million and several transport planes. President Clinton promised a "vigorous" approach to solving the problem. One might ask how this was possible when something as small as the use of troop carriers was so vigorously debated only a few months previously. There were a couple of reasons. First, the plight of the refugees in the camps was widely covered by the media, and second, sending aid could not embroil the United States in a political controversy. They were not supplying or transporting troops, so there could be no repeat of the Somalia fiasco.

Sabotaged Census

When the former government people running the camps realized that the amount of aid that came under their control was dependent upon the number of people living in the camps, they had another, more material reason for keeping the people there. In fact, the truth is that no one knew exactly how many people were in the Zaire camps, because the people in charge of the camps sabotaged every attempt at a thorough census.

The former Hutu Power elite who ran the camps knew that inflating the numbers led to extra rations. With this in mind they also encouraged pregnancy in the camps and reported a birth rate that approached the limit of human capacity. The goal was to breed more Hutus, and any pregnancy, even forced impregnation (rape), was regarded as a public service among the Interahamwe. Similarly, any attempt to leave the camps and return home to Rwanda was considered an act of treason.

As a result, a good many of the million and a half people living in the camps were actually hostages. Though they were told by the people running the camps that certain death awaited them in Rwanda, the vast majority were at no risk of being jailed, much less killed, in Rwanda. Officially, the UNHCR promoted "voluntary repatriation" in the border camps. In the beginning, this was done by people signing up a day or two in advance for buses that would take them back to Rwanda.

After a number of the people who signed up were killed before their departure dates, it was decided to station idling buses outside the camps every morning and let people make a run for them. When no one did, this program was also abandoned. The old Hutu Power mixture of propaganda and brute force was still effective.

Need for the Camps

There is no question that in the beginning the camps were needed. Without refuge, hundreds of thousands more would have died. And even though the average Hutu was not facing slaughter by the RPF as they were being told, there were still good reasons to not go home. First, they would carry the cholera back into the hills of Rwanda, where it might never be contained. Second, it would be almost impossible to weed out the ex-RGF troops and Interhamwe militia, and they would continue to wreak havoc in Rwanda. Third, there was no new government in place in Rwanda, and if the old *bourgmestres* and prefects returned to their areas, they would grab for power, and the people would obey them, creating a whole new set of problems. The camps were necessary, but the good they provided was slowly being overrun by the evil they harbored.

What made the camps so bizarre was the twisted juxtaposition of hundreds of aid workers trying to do their best for humanity, right next to a large group of individuals who were guilty of—and still performing—horrendous crimes against humanity.

The World Begins to Notice

As the RPF took more and more of Rwanda, the soldiers discovered one new horror after another. The army captured fields of corpses; the rivers overflowed with bodies. Finally, the world was starting to realize what had happened in Rwanda. The former government denied it, and in a typical broadcast at the end of June, RTLMC announcer Georges Ruggiu proclaimed:

"The fifty thousand bodies that can be found in Lake Victoria, which threaten Lake Victoria with pollution—they come from massacres which only the RPF could have committed."

These people had not been killed by the RPF. There was no denying the truth in Uganda, where fifty thousand bodies could be seen floating, hacked to death by machetes. Although the RPF radio had been reporting the massacres, and people in neighboring nations heard RTLMC celebrating the deaths, no one believed it was to this extent. There had not been many Tutsi refugees who escaped Rwanda to talk about the genocide. Generally, a crisis in Africa is quickly followed by a large mass of refugees crossing the borders into other countries to tell the story, but the roadblocks had done their job. In every village, on every road, on every path, people had been placed to call people to come and kill anyone they saw walking or hiding in the bushes.

Coming across the Ugandan border were the UN soldiers and their trucks and equipment being shipped back at the command of the United Nations. The UN had been dramatically reducing its force since the killing of the ten Belgian soldiers. They were afraid General Dallaire would act on his own, so they incapacitated him by removing the army.

Return to Rwanda

I had heard the radio broadcasts, but now I saw the bodies and the UN running away, and I knew the worst had happened. The world had turned its back, and my people had been slaughtered. I began to pray and ask God what He wanted me to do now.

By the end of July, it was all I could think about. Those of us in Uganda could no longer eat fish, because the dead bodies had polluted the lake, and the fish had fed on them. I couldn't stop thinking that some of those dead bodies were no doubt people I had known—men, women, and even children—and now they were floating dead in the lake, and no one had done anything to stop it. It was then I realized that I had to go back to Rwanda.

I wasn't sure what I could do, but I knew I could do something, so I put together a group of eleven pastors, and we rented a minibus. I felt we needed to see for ourselves what they were calling a genocide. I remember telling the other pastors, "If God is going to use us, we need to go there and see this for ourselves. If we are going to preach God again there, we don't need to be told by anyone what happened. We must see it for ourselves."

What we saw was horrifying. There were corpses everywhere; sometimes they'd been reduced to skeletons by the dogs and the vultures, and always, there was the stench of rotting flesh.

In *Shake Hands with the Devil,* Roméo Dallaire described the conditions in the countryside this way:

> We drove through village after deserted village, some still smouldering. Garbage, rags and bodies intermingled at places where either an ambush or a massacre had occurred. We drove by abandoned checkpoints ringed with corpses, sometimes beheaded and dumped like rubbish, sometimes stacked meticulously beside neat piles of heads. Many corpses rapidly decayed into blinding white skeletons in the hot sun . . .
>
> For a long time I completely wiped the death masks of raped and sexually mutilated girls and women from my mind as if what had been done to them was the last thing that would send me over the edge. But if you looked, you could see the evidence, even in the whitened skeletons. The legs bent and apart. A broken bottle, a rough branch, even a knife between them . . . There was always a lot of blood . . . It was the expressions on their dead faces that assaulted me the most, a frieze of shock, pain and humiliation.[5]

In the same book Dallaire described a particularly grisly scene.

> I did not want to risk our vehicles on the bridge. As we made our way across on foot, I noticed that clothes were caught between the struts of the floating base and I stopped to look over the side. Staring up at me were the faces of half-nude corpses, stuck under the bridge. There were a lot of them. In some

places they had accumulated to the point that we were actually walking on a bridge of dead bodies.[6]

This was the Rwanda to which we came. The RPF had taken Ruhengari and Gisenyi, and they were still fighting around Kibuye. We came in from the east and stayed at a military camp in Gaheni. We went to Yamata and saw mass graves, where the heads were peeping out of the ground. They had tied them together at the hip and brought in a Caterpillar to cover their bodies. We saw three huge mass graves before they collected the bodies and reburied them into the memorial graves that we have today.

From Yamata we went to different places. Everywhere we would see bodies. Sometimes they were mixed with the bodies of dead dogs or cats, because the enemy would break into a home and kill everything there. It was very awful, and that visit was extremely hard. Three of the pastors with me on the trip were traumatized. They went sort of crazy for a few days.

The guide who took us was also traumatized. We were visiting a home where there were twenty-seven dead bodies around and inside it, and the guide threw up. I had to pick her up and carry her back to the car. I left her in the car and then returned and took pictures. The RPF gave us a guide because the government had mined some of the roads to hinder the RPF's progress, and the RPF had already demined paths through and around them.

It was important for me to experience these things, especially if I was going to help the people of Rwanda recover. That's why I encourage visitors to our country to visit the memorial sites, so they will understand that we are dealing with some of the heaviest and hardest burdens that a human being, a human soul, can ever carry. When you visit Nyamata, or go to Ntarama, and see twenty-four rooms filled with dead bodies, you get some idea of the pain this country suffered. You can see babies and children still fastened together with adults. Skeletons with their skin dried over them. Some of them still have hair on them. That's why we preach about Jesus, who can restore the dead to life—Jesus who can restore life to the nation of Rwanda.

The End of the Genocide:
Welcome to the Wasteland

On July 18, the RPF took Gisenyi after an intensive artillery battle. They immediately began securing the northwest border with Zaire. That same day Paul Kagame founded a new government in Kigali, and General Augustin Bizimungu, the RGF chief of staff safely tucked away in Goma, stated, "The RPF will rule over a desert." Not only were the people leaving, but the interim government also had taken everything of value that they could get their hands on when they left Kigali. They took all the Central Bank foreign currency reserves, as well as very large amounts of cash in Rwandese francs. Every fixed installation that could be destroyed was destroyed before they left. Most of the infrastructures had been brutally looted, with door and window frames removed, and electric switches pried from walls. Just about every decent running vehicle, except RPF military ones, had been driven over the border to Zaire. Not a penny had been left in the public treasury.

There was no running water and electricity in the towns, and although the crops on the hills were ripe, nobody was left to harvest them. Those Tutsis who came out of hiding or returned from exile found empty pastures aplenty to feed their cows. The goal had been to leave behind only a wasteland to the victorious RPF, and it had been pretty much accomplished.

During the previous three months, more than 10 percent of the population had been killed and another 30 percent had gone into exile.[7] Those left in Rwanda were in a complete state of disarray. Most were displaced, and a large number had lost everything. There were a few Tutsis still hiding in the hills, and now many Hutus, afraid of the RPF, had joined them. The French Zone Turquoise provided some stability in the southwest for about 1.2 million people, mostly Hutus, but most of the rest of the country lived in a state of fear, either paralyzed by guilt or traumatized by loss.

On July 19, the new government was sworn in at Kigali. It was essentially a coalition between the RPF and the few surviving members of Hutu Power opposition parties. Pasteur Bizimungu, the oldest of the Hutus who had been sympathetic to the RPF, was appointed president, and Paul Kagame was appointed vice president.

The cabinet had a Hutu majority fitting the breakdown of the population, sixteen of the twenty-two positions. Since the government offices had been stripped by the departing Hutu Power advocates, most of the new ministers didn't even have a typewriter, much less an office or a secretary, but their appointment did provide a strong indication of the new government's intentions.

The United States had withdrawn their diplomatic recognition of Rwanda's former government on the fifteenth and shut down its Washington embassy, and now in New York, the United Nations ambassador from Rwanda, a member of the ousted regime, was forced to give up his seat on the Security Council. Paul Kagame and the RPF had won—and they, perhaps with the aid of God, but certainly without any help from the rest of the world, had stopped the genocide.

Since the end of May the killings had been more sporadic and less systematic, but that was primarily because the large groups of Tutsis in the cities and villages had been wiped out, and all that were left were isolated pockets of survivors caught in their hiding places. The typhoon of madness that swept through the country between April 7 and the third week of May accounted for 80 percent of the victims of the genocide.

That means about eight hundred thousand people were murdered during those six weeks, making the daily killing rate at least five times that of the Nazi death camps. The simple peasants of Rwanda, with their machetes, clubs, and sticks with nails, had killed at a faster rate than the Nazi death machine with its gas chambers, mass ovens, and firing squads. In my opinion, the killing frenzy of the Rwandan genocide shared a vital common thread with the technological efficiency of the Nazi genocide—satanic hate in abundance was at the core of both.

EIGHT

Machetes into Plowshares

The End of Operation Turquoise

On August 21, 1994, the French left Rwanda. There were 1.5 million people living in the Zone Turquoise by this time, and only another 3.2 million living in the rest of the country. The effects of the genocide and the resulting exodus had cut the country's population almost in half. Despite their clear favoritism toward helping the former government and their Hutu Power allies, the French provided some very necessary sanctuary for many Rwandans. So much so, in fact, that half a million people left the country for Bakavu in Zaire in the few weeks before the French departed.

The World's Perception of the Refugee Camps

In yet another bizarre twist of fate, the first time most of the world got a real glimpse of the massive human suffering that occurred in Rwanda in 1994 was through the media coverage of the refugee camps. Off and on for months, people heard that something horrible was happening in Rwanda. At first the media talked about a civil war; then it became clear that a genocide had taken place. And now CNN and most other news programs were airing video footage concerning Rwanda. But what they showed was the pain and anguish of the refugee camps.

More than a million displaced persons suffering from malaria and cholera were herded into sparse refugee camps and depended on foreign aid for survival. Naturally, viewers assumed that this was the tragedy of Rwanda. The world saw images of the suffering Rwandan, and they were moved to help. The aid began pouring in. Very few people understood that the real tragedy of Rwanda was a million dead Tutsis—there had been no television coverage of that. In modern society, if a catastrophe isn't shown on the television news, it doesn't exist.

The world felt sorry for the huddled masses in the camps, but no one told them that the same men who helped to engineer the torturous deaths of a million men, women, and children were running the camps. No one talked about the cause of the malaria epidemic—people living and eating near piles of corpses. No one mentioned that the persecution of the innocent in the form of beatings, rapes, and murders was not only continuing in the camps, but being supported and paid for by the rest of the world.

By late August 1994, even the United Nations High Commissioner for Refugees admitted to the problems. Ray Wilkinson, a UNHCR official stated flatly, "We are in a state of virtual war in the camps."[1]

No matter what the camps looked like on television, they were, in fact, functioning as major Hutu Power military installations. The ex-RGF soldiers and Interahamwe militia operated a reign of terror—stealing, raping, and killing virtually at random. When they wanted something, they took it. That included everything from international aid to young peasant girls.

The same forces controlled the airfields, which meant that landing alongside the UNICEF and Red Cross planes were planes full of guns and ammo. The former government leaders flew in and out of the camps, meeting with the RGF and the Interahamwe, issuing orders and then flying back to safety in Nairobi or some other place of refuge.

While the corruption in the camps was largely unreported, the suffering of the people living there became a staple on the nightly news around the world.

Though most viewers had no idea what the real issues in Rwanda had been, those few who did know could not escape the bizarre twist of justice they were viewing. The killers of Rwanda's Tutsis were now dying horrible deaths of their own.

Secretary General of *Medecins Sans Frontieres,* Alain Destexhe, put it this way:

> Yesterday the genocide of the Tutsi by the Hutu militia, today the genocide of the Hutu refugees by the cholera? This comparison, which one can see widely used in the press, puts on the same plane things that have nothing to do with each other. Through this confusion the original, singular, and exemplary nature of the genocide is denied and the guilt of the perpetrators becomes diluted in the general misery.

Watering Down and Mocking the Truth

The truth was that the grievous impact of the genocide was being watered down and washed away by the much-covered suffering in the refugee camps. The concept of divine retribution being applied to the terrible sufferings of the Hutu refugees in Goma weakened the intensity of feeling toward the genocide. The genocide became part of the general misery and never received the proper recognition on the world stage. This allowed the United Nations and the rest of the international community to escape the public outcry that the ignoring of the genocide deserved. The media coverage couldn't have worked out better if it had been planned—or was it?

As the discovery of corpses in Rwanda continued, the Hutu Power organizations took their most ludicrous stance yet by actually claiming the Tutsis had drowned themselves and committed suicide because they felt so bad about the RPF attacking the country. Not only were such statements totally irresponsible, but they were cruelly mocking the truth and heaped more suffering upon the few surviving Tutsis. For them to hear such things on the radio or read them in the Hutu Power–controlled newspapers was psychological torture to those few who had survived the genocide. They mocked the dead.

Attacks from the Camps

For the *genocidaires* the plan had been to use the camps as a place to regroup and form a new attack strategy. It was no surprise to most Rwandans that they soon began using the camps as a base from which to launch new attacks on the Tutsis of Rwanda. The rivers and lakes near the camps provided strategic natural barriers. Consequently, the Interahamwe could send out raiding parties without fear of reprisal in kind. Squads of militia and ex-RGF troops came down from the mountains in Uganda or out of the jungles near Lake Kivu, where most of the population was Hutu.

Sometimes they ventured into Rwanda and attacked the remaining Tutsis or those who had come back home thinking it was safe. Other times they attacked the Tutsis who lived near the camps in the very country providing them sanctuary. They buried caches of guns and other weapons all around these areas for just this purpose. All the RPF could do was hope to catch them in the act. The only other option was to launch a full-fledged attack on an internationally protected refugee camp.

Mokoto Monastery "Cleansing"

One of the worst of these attacks was on a monastery in the village of Mokoto, which had taken in hundreds of refugee Tutsis. By early 1996, some of the financial support by the Western nations for the refugee camps was beginning to wane, and there was talk that they might have to close. The Hutu Power advocates decided to "cleanse" the mountainous regions of North Kivu and attacked Tutsi villages in this area.

Many of the survivors of these attacks were now living at the monastery run by Father Dhelo. The monks there ran six schools and a dispensary, providing most of the social services for Mokoto and other neighboring villages. When the local Hutus threatened him for providing sanctuary to the Tutsis, the brave priest faced them and offered to die if necessary for the lives of the Tutsis.

In early May of 1996, Father Dhelo went away on business. A thousand Tutsi refugees were camped outside the church when a large mob of Hutus surrounded them on the evening of May 8. When shots were fired into the air, the Tutsis ran for the church. On Friday the monastery was warned that a major attack was about to begin. By Sunday morning, the last of the monks had fled on a tractor. Soon afterward the Hutus pushed their way into the church and began dragging people out and killing them with machetes. More than a hundred died.

In Philip Gourevitch's award-winning book, *We Wish to Inform You That Tomorrow We Will Be Killed with Our Families,* he described the results of the Mokoto massacre:

> A few days before I arrived in Kitchanga, a relief team from Doctors Without Borders had driven up to the Mokoto monastery and found the road blocked by two charred, naked corpses; the hands, feet, and genitals had been cut off, the chests had been opened, and the hearts had been removed . . . they estimated the dead to number at least a hundred. While they were at the monastery, some wounded Tutsis came out of the bush where they had been hiding. One was a naked boy who had contrived to cover only the back of his neck. When he let the covering fall away, they saw that his head had been cut almost halfway off, exposing his spine and a patch of cranium. A doctor had sewed the boy back together, and I saw him walking tentatively around an emergency field hospital at Kitchanga.
>
> A barefoot man in a tattered raincoat and shorts at the village school, who identified himself as "the captain of the Mokoto refugees," said that many of the attackers had come from the UN camps. It was very easy to identify them, he said, because "they spoke excellent Kinyarwanda and were well dressed . . ."
>
> The captain told me that the Hutu Power militias at Mokoto had chanted, "Kill, kill, kill," and "This is how we fled our country." Unlike the Zairean Tutsi refugees I had met in Rwanda, who said their only hope was to return to Zaire, the captain of the Mokoto Tutsis had given up.[2]

Ironically, the Tutsis being chased out of North Kivu by such massacres wound up seeking refuge in Rwanda. The new Rwandan government accused Zaire of complicity, since their troops had often driven Tutsis to the border and then taken away or destroyed their Zairean citizenship papers. As 1996 wore on, the attacks from the camps grew fiercer. So many original genocide survivors were killed that the African Rights organization claimed that the Hutu Power advocates were "killing the evidence." By the end of August 1996, North Kivu had been effectively "cleansed."

Propaganda Poisons New Generation

Not only were continued attacks on Tutsis coming from the Hutu refugee camps, but anti-Tutsi propaganda also flourished there, poisoning a new generation of Hutus. Aid workers in the camps reported that the children had a game where they would make tiny clay figures and put them in the road. When a passing vehicle would run over and crush one, the children cheered, claiming that they had just caused a Tutsi to die in Rwanda.

Kagame's Plea for the Refugees

As the problems in the camps continued to build, Paul Kagame became more and more concerned. In July 1996, he went to Washington, D.C., to personally articulate to United States representatives why the refugee camps were such a problem. His parting statement was that if the international community couldn't get the camps under control, he would find a way to do it himself.

There were some in the new government who questioned why Kagame so strongly advocated the return of the people in the camps. After all, they were all Hutus, and that could only undermine any power the Tutsis had, and, even more importantly, many of the people in the camps had killed innocent Tutsi families, and some of them would try to start trouble again the moment they returned. "We want [the] people back," he said at the time, "because it is their right and . . . our responsibility to have them back, whether they support us or not."[3]

Nightmare in Zaire

By now Kagame had established a fairly strong military presence throughout the country, and the attacks from the camps into Rwanda were sporadic at best.

Instead, the Hutu Power people running the camps took their unspoken alliance with President Mobuto of Zaire to the next step. As Kagame suspected, once North Kivu had been cleared of Tutsis, the focus was on South Kivu. Around four hundred thousand Tutsis lived in the region. They were known as the Banyamulenge (the people of Mulenge), because Mulenge was where their ancestors had settled after migrating from Rwanda some two hundred years before.

Since the founding of the refugee camps, their cattle had been raided, and anti-Tutsi propaganda began showing up in local newspapers and on radio stations. Already the Zairean officials were scheming to take their land and calling them "snakes." The attacks began in September 1996 and included not only the Hutu Power people from the camps but also locally recruited militia and even some Mobutist forces. Homes were burned; people were arrested or deported to Rwanda. Some were lynched in the streets under the approving eye of government officials. The nightmare was beginning again.

A major difference between the Tutsis in North and South Kivu was that the southerners were armed. The Banyamulenge had the means and the will to fight back. Added to this were resistance fighters, trained and equipped in Rwanda, no doubt Kagame's way to unofficially participate. Although the aid workers made no public protests, they were aware enough of the violence to evacuate the area as the fighting intensified. More and more the Zairean government was participating one way or another in the persecutions of the Banyamulenge Tutsi.

As the death toll began to rise, the situation looked more and more like the genocide all over again. In Kigali, Paul Kagame seethed. "We were ready to hit them [Zaire]," he told Gourevitch, "hit them very hard—and handle three things: first to save the Banyamulenge and not let them die, empower them to fight, and even fight for them; then to dismantle the camps, return the refugees to Rwanda, and destroy the ex-Far [RGF] and militias; and, third, to change the situation in Zaire."[4]

But Kagame dared not risk the international outcry if he intervened before sufficient provocation. On October 8, 1996, he got it. Lwasi Ngabo Lwabanji, the deputy governor of South Kivu, announced that the Banyamulenge Tutsis were exiled. They had one week to leave the country. After that they would be considered rebels in a state of war with Zaire, and the entire Zairean army could be brought against them.

No doubt Lwasi made this pronouncement without consulting Mobutu, who was then undergoing treatment for prostate cancer in Switzerland. It was not the kind of official statement Mobutu would have approved. Zaire wanted the Tutsis out, but deputy governors don't issue such sweeping declarations. Even so, it was all Kagame needed, and he attacked with everything he had. The Banyamulenge joined with him, and the Alliance of Democratic Forces for the Liberation of Congo / Zaire, Laurent Kabila's rebel force, joined in the fray.

The Zairean army were known for their lack of commitment, and they immediately fled. The aid workers were evacuated and the camps dispersed. By November 2 the combined liberation forces took Goma and Kabila and announced that an area of a thousand square miles was now "liberated." Playing it safe, Kagame denied Rwanda's involvement (until admitting it in June 1997), but he was openly pleased.

The march through Zaire was halted when ex-RGF and Interahamwe militias herded 750,000 refugees into the lava fields in and around the Mugunga camp to block their progress. Kabila appealed to the humanitarian organizations to get the refugees out of harm's way. Nothing happened, and soon news of people dying from disease and starvation began to surface. Some reports claimed tens of thousands had died. Others said a hundred thousand. United Nations Secretary General Boutros-Ghali suddenly announced that "genocide by starvation" was taking place outside Mugunga.[5] While this was highly doubtful, no one could prove otherwise.

The UN began preparing to send in troops who, not being allowed to use force, would have no power to do anything. Things were looking very bad. No one would act. And then Paul Kagame stepped in. Ordering his RPA (the newly named Rwandan Patriotic Army) to circle back behind Mugunga and attack from the rear, he was able to draw the Hutu Power forces away from the refugees and at the same time send the refugees in the direction of Rwanda.

Soon the Hutu Power militias retreated deeper into Zaire to join the fleeing Zairean army in the jungles.

The Return of the Refugees

The refugees came home to Rwanda. And they came in great numbers, not only those who had been freed from Zaire, but also Hutus and Tutsis in exile from every bordering nation. One estimate was that two hundred people a minute were entering Rwanda—that's twelve thousand every hour. The final ploy of the Hutu Power advocates—to leave Rwanda a nation without a population—had been overcome. Paul Kagame rejoiced. In a welcoming home speech, he called the mass return "a tremendous joy for all Rwandans," and then went on to say, "The Rwandan people were able to live together peacefully for six hundred years and there is no reason why they can't live together in peace again."[6]

Kagame also spoke to the killers: "Let me appeal to those who have chosen the murderous and confrontational path, by reminding them that they, too, are Rwandans. I am calling upon you to abandon your genocidal and destructive ways, join hands with other Rwandans, and put that energy to better use. . . . Once again welcome home."[7]

Kagame was wise in addressing those who had participated in the genocide. Everyone knew that the split between those who had followed the Interahamwe into the jungles of Zaire and those who had joined the ranks of the returning refugees was not a perfect one. Many of the innocent had chosen Zaire, and many of the killers had chosen Rwanda. Kagame knew that there would be more killings—some a continuation of the forces that triggered the genocide and some a retaliation for it. There would have to be prosecutions as well.

The ignorant peasants who had been manipulated by fear and propaganda and sometimes even forced to commit crimes were one thing, but the organizers, the manipulators, the propagandists, and those who forced others to kill—they must be arrested and tried. But the people were together now, and that was a start. All that was needed was a miracle to reconcile them.

Relocating to Rwanda

After my visit to Rwanda in August 1994, I never stopped working toward reconciliation. While in Uganda, I began organizing conferences of church leaders in Rwanda. I tried to encourage them to come together again and rediscover themselves, discover who they were in God. No matter how horrible things had been, God remains God. Any church leader who saw Rwanda in August 1994 knew that he or she needed to go back to work.

By 1996, I was feeling called to become part of this community—the new Rwandan church. I thought at first that I would just increase the conferences I was running and maybe begin a few crusades, encouraging people to come to the Lord Jesus Christ and repent. For a while I thought I could do that best from Uganda. I had a large ministry in Uganda, a very good home, and I had land. My children were going to good schools. I had everything that a man wants to be firmly established in a place.

Uganda had granted me citizenship, and it's very rare in Africa for a refugee to get citizenship. Usually, once you become a refugee, your children become refugees, and your grandchildren become refugees. It was a rare gift for me to have that citizenship. But in 1997, a group of people from Shyira diocese wrote me a letter saying, "John, we know you. You are the son of John Baptist Kabango and he was the son of Ntampuhwe" and so on, tracing my lineage. They said, "You are Rwandan. We need you. Rwanda needs you."

And at first I replied, "No, I don't think I should come back", but something inside me said maybe, so I asked them to "let me consider it." They wrote another letter and said, "You know what the Bible said about Jonah going to Ninevah. You may think you are comfortable in Uganda and you may not want to respond because the comfort may be a temptation to you. Be careful. Go and pray, but this is what we see as your temptation."

Moments of doubts are part of life, and they are part of the Christian walk as well. It's what you do with them that matters. Coming back to Rwanda was a huge thing for me to consider, something that I really had to put to the Lord in prayer. I had many doubts. My friends told me I was silly to think about leaving a flourishing ministry in Uganda to come to a country of violence, and how it was especially unwise to think about bringing my family, which was very stabilized in Uganda, into that violence. There was no assurance, no guarantee that I would be alive even a week after I returned.

In the northwestern area where I was thinking about moving, the perpetrators of the genocide were infiltrating back into the country and killing people. They killed a Roman Catholic priest near where I was going. Being part of the clergy meant even less than it had during the genocide. A lot of people didn't trust the clergy any longer, and rightly so. There were risks. And these risks gave me moments of doubt.

But every time I slowed down and prayed, I heard a voice. I heard a clear encouragement from within me that Rwanda needed to hear a new message of hope, and those who were violent could not preach that message. Somebody had to stand in the middle of them and preach about hope. God was challenging me to be one of the people who preached that message. I began dreaming about all the projects that were needed in Rwanda and then I knew—I had to go.

Willing to Serve

I contacted the people who had been requesting me to come and told them that I would, but I didn't know in what capacity. I didn't want to get involved in church politics. I had no stomach for that kind of thing as related to this issue. They proposed that I be a candidate to become a bishop. I said that if it was the will of God that I was elected bishop, I would serve. But I would not get involved in church politics. I could not be a good witness for Jesus if I had to campaign for an election. They said, "That's not your responsibility. We just want you to say yes, you're accepting to serve."

I said, "Yes, I will."

I told the bishop in Uganda that I was going to transfer my service to Rwanda. He didn't want to lose me, but he knew the gravity of the need. Still, he asked me to consider staying. The mission work we were doing in Uganda was wonderful, and people were being saved all over the country. I had trained two lay evangelists to work with me in organizing preaching crusades. I would collect the lay evangelists and all those who would witness for Jesus and put them on a truck and send them out to different communities. They would preach for a week and then crown it on Sunday by having the people who had accepted Jesus that week celebrate at the church.

In the end, the bishop said he didn't want to lose me, but he had to consider and compare the need. He said, "Maybe it's the will of God, because they need you more." So he let me go, and he gave me a good recommendation. I moved back to Rwanda in 1996, and on June 8, 1997, they consecrated me Bishop of Shyira diocese, which covers Ruhengeri, Gisenyi, and Kibuye provinces.

Guerrilla Warfare

This area, like most of Rwanda at the time, was in a state of fear and confusion. When the camps were dismantled, the ex-RGF soldiers and Interahamwe militia ran into the jungles, which gave them a perfect setting to conduct guerrilla warfare. They would strike and run. Usually they came over the border from the mountains in the Congo jungles and killed at random. They killed the villagers because the villagers were loyal to the new government and were not supporting the old government forces when they returned.

These forces wanted to overthrow the Kagame government, and they thought that because they were Hutu, the Hutu population would support them. They didn't understand that the Hutus were beginning to conceive that government should not be about just Hutu or Tutsi; it should be about having a sound, healthy society, a healthy economy, a healthy population, and a healthy nation.

Family Tragedy

Shortly after I was consecrated as bishop, my niece, Madu, came to visit me. She was sixteen years old, and she came to tell me that her mother, sister, and brother wanted to move away from their town to near where we lived, but they would need help. They felt unsafe where they were living, because they were a mixed family. Madu's father was a Tutsi and her mother a Hutu, and the rebels were coming over the border into their area all the time. She was afraid that they might pick them out and harm them.

I told her that I would take care of the provisions for the move, and they should come immediately. She thanked me and went back home to make preparations for the move. The same evening she arrived home, infiltrators attacked. They held Madu down and took their machetes and peeled the flesh off both her arms from the shoulder to the wrist, and then they stripped her naked and raped her while she was in that pain. After they raped her, they cut her neck and slaughtered her. They killed her mother, brother, and sister too.

Early the next morning, some Christians from her area came out of hiding and brought the news to us. We made burial arrangements, but the soldiers would not let me attend the funeral, because they said that if a bishop came, it would attract public attention, and many more people would die. It was a tragic and devastating moment for my family and me. We mourned in silence. It was very painful for my children, especially my daughters who were near her age and very close to her. They could not conceive—none of us could—the pain this dear girl went through. To me, it was yet another example of how the devil penetrated the hearts of the killers in Rwanda. We deeply grieve the loss to this day.

Dangerous Travel

Most of the time it was very difficult to go to Kigali for meetings, because those who continued to advocate violence would attack cars along the road. One time they bombed a number of minibuses that were just ahead of us, and they killed twenty people. We found warm, bleeding, dead bodies, and others on the verge of death. Blood was flowing in the middle of the road. One of the minibuses was still burning, and the flames were high.

Another time they shot eight bullets at my car from the hills, but missed us. Then another time, I could see some men coming down the side of the hill toward the road, with military guns in their hands. I told the priest driving the car to speed up. We were able to drive past them before they could shoot, but the van behind us was intercepted, and five people were killed. They couldn't put up checkpoints, because the new army was patrolling, so they just hid until they saw a car coming down the road and then hit it, killed people, and ran away.

It didn't matter who was in the cars. They didn't care. They just wanted to spread fear and undermine the confidence people had in the new government. They wanted people to know that the government was not able to control them. They wanted to be a threat so they could have power over the people.

A Bishop's Calling

Why would anybody want to be enthroned as a bishop in a situation like that? I felt God was saying, *If you do not go there and present the healing gospel, then the fate of Rwanda will be in the hands of those who carry guns. If God is the remedy and the solution, whom shall He use, if you don't allow Him to use you?* I knew that it all made sense, considering my background and history.

God did not remove me from my school and my country. But He would use and turn to good what the devil and the people who intended evil did to me. Even as I was exiled, God was preparing me through the suffering and through that hopeless situation. God saved me from that lostness and prepared me through pain and through the wilderness of mind and experience. He prepared me for a ministry of reconciliation in the center of the brokenness of Rwanda. This was my calling.

The Return of the Exiles

Another astonishing aspect of Rwanda's story is how the Tutsi exiles returned to their country—not the refugees of the genocide, but people who left long before it began, some as early as 1959. For thirty-five years Tutsis had been persecuted in Rwanda, forcing 336,000 to flee the country by 1964. By 1993 that number had grown to 600,000. But after the RPF victory in July of 1994, they began to return home. And they brought their families with them, so that before a year had passed following the RPF victory, more than 700,000 Tutsis had returned to Rwanda.

Today that number has grown to more than a million. For every Tutsi who was killed in the genocide, another one returned to the country from exile, so that the total number of Tutsis living in Rwanda is almost the same as it was before the genocide.

Part of the reason for the return of these exiles was that the countries they immigrated to never fully embraced them. But much of it was also the sincere longing that the exiled had for their homeland. Even those who prospered in other countries always said they longed to be in Rwanda and at times seemed to be overwhelmed by feelings of rootlessness.

Faustin Gesgona's family fled Rwanda in 1960. He returned from Burundi in 1995. "The situation in Burundi has become unbearable," he said at the time, "but even if it wasn't I would return to Rwanda. This is where my family will live now that the RPF is in charge."

Dr. Fred Tagwa came from Uganda. His parents fled the Tutsi persecutions of 1959, and when he returned to Gitarma in 1995, it was the first time he had seen Rwanda. "My parents come from villages in the hills, but I'm looking to settle my family here."

Even Kagame and the new government were somewhat surprised by the number of exiles who returned. A great many of these people had never before set foot in Rwanda, and now many were abandoning possessions and lands— to say nothing of safety and security—in order to settle in a country that had been ravaged by the genocide of their own people.

The difficulties of exile and the longing for their homeland no doubt played significant roles in this return, but there was something more—a determination to defy the undefiable. Perhaps nothing seems as complete and final as the idea of genocide, and now these people were standing up to be counted as challengers to that finality. The Tutsi would survive. Rwanda would survive. They would make certain of it.

The Scars

Rwanda in 1997 was a huge, festering wound that had to be carefully treated if the patient was to survive. Everywhere there were the devastating effects of the genocide. There were 114,000 children without parents. In many cases they were traumatized children who had watched the gruesome murders of their parents, brothers, sisters, and other family members.

Dallaire described his visit to an orphanage:

> One orphanage in the Butare area still harboured over six hundred children .. . Many of the kids were so psychologically damaged that they were immobile, sitting here, there and everywhere and reacting to nothing, even the hundreds of flies that clustered at every orifice of their bruised, dirty and frail bodies. The eyes in their thin faces seemed to blaze at you like lasers, projecting beams of energy that burned right into your heart.[8]

A UNICEF study found that five out of six children who had been in Rwanda during the genocide had, at the very least, witnessed bloodshed. Studies on domestic violence have indicated that 30 percent of children who witness violence in their home later become perpetrators of violence, as compared to 3 percent of the general population. But when children have been exposed to the kind of traumatic events that happened during the genocide, there are all kinds of other stress reactions that may occur, such as abnormal aggressiveness, strong mood swings, nightmares, eating disturbances, learning problems, repeated fainting, vague aches and pains, loss of speech and of bladder and bowel control, and clinging to (or withdrawal from) adults.

Some children who lived through the Rwanda genocide blame themselves for it, while some blame themselves for surviving or feel it would have been better to have been killed with their families. Many of them live with a sense of helplessness and hopelessness. What makes things even more difficult is that these symptoms of psychological distress may not be apparent to adults, especially to an uneducated population. If the child's behavior is not understood as a reaction to stress, parents or caretaking adults may punish or reject the child. Severe reactions, such as loss of speech and bladder control, might even be interpreted as mental retardation.

If five out of six children living in Rwanda during the genocide witnessed bloodshed, what are the figures for adults? No one who lived through the genocide escaped damage. There were innumerable men, women, and children with missing limbs and other horrible scars. But the level of psychic damage was even greater. Anyone who saw his friends and relatives tortured and killed, but escaped physical harm himself, carried an unexplainable guilt, usually accompanied by horrible nightmares equaled in terror only by the actual memories. The terror of Rwanda did not stop with the end of the genocide.

The victims were not the only ones who were scarred. The killers, too, carried horrible memories that haunted them by day and attacked them in their dreams at night. And for some, the hardening of their hearts toward suffering left them with no conscience, no hesitation to cause pain to others, such as the man who set a girl on fire at a Kigali disco because she wouldn't dance with him. She told him to go away, and he came back with a can of gasoline and set her on fire.

Four people were killed, and the assailant was hospitalized with burns. When they asked why he did it, he said it was nothing to him after what he'd done in 1994—he could kill as many as he liked. And what about the young boys who were taken from their schools to help with the genocide? They lost their futures. Now, after ten years in jail, where do you put them? Much of that generation is lost unless God heals them.

Rwanda was fortunate that starvation didn't follow the genocide, as it has elsewhere. The ground in Rwanda is extremely fertile. That, along with the people's ability to make do with less, is what prevented a famine. People simply made do with what they had.

Integration of Returning Exiles and Genocide Survivors

Another huge problem was the integration of Tutsis who survived the genocide in Rwanda with those returning from exile. Although a person might think the two groups had a great deal in common, the experience of watching your family,

friends, and neighbors being wiped out by the thousands is so unique and so terrible that nothing compares to it, not even leaving one's home for another country to avoid it. A Tutsi who did not wish to be identified said:

> We survivors find it very difficult to integrate into the present society
> and—I hate to say it—into the government, too. They have their own
> style from outside, and they don't have much trust in us either. When
> they came they took the country as in a conquest. They thought it was
> theirs to look after. They said of us Tutsis who were here, "The smart
> ones are dead and those who survived are traumatized." The young RPF
> fighters all had their parents coming from outside the country and they
> were tired of the austerity of fighting, so they took homes and goods for
> their families and they didn't like the survivors getting in the way.
>
> And they would say, "If they killed everyone and you survived, maybe
> you collaborated." To a woman who was raped twenty times a day, day
> after day, and now has a baby from that, they would say this. To a Tutsi
> who was intermarried or a child who was orphaned they would say this.
> Can you imagine? For us, it was too hard at first, finding that everyone
> was dead, that we didn't know anyone. It didn't occur to us to grab bet-
> ter houses, and now it's we who are taking care of most of the orphans.[9]

There were many women who had been raped during the genocide and now
had unwanted children. As time went on, there were many survivors who were
now returning to live among the killers of their families. In *We Wish to Inform
You That Tomorrow We Will Be Killed with Our Families,* a survivor named
Odette is quoted. She had a nephew who survived the genocide in Kinunu, on
the hill where she was born in Gisenyi. She had visited him only once, to help
bury the dead, who were numerous, and she did not want to go back.

> All the Hutus there watched us come, and some wanted to hug me . . . I cried
> out, "Don't touch me. Where did you put everyone?" One was married to a
> cousin of mine. I said, "Where's Therese?" . . . He said, "It wasn't me who did

it." I said, "I don't want to see you. I don't want to know you." . . . People will say I'm an extremist because I can't accept or tolerate the people who killed my family. So if they're afraid once in their lives—I was afraid since I was three years old—let them know how it feels.[10]

Laurencie Nyirabeza told author Philip Gourevitch her feelings about one of the killers who had returned to her community:

A certain Girumuhatse is back, a man who beat me during the war with a stick, and from who I received a machete blow also. This man threw me in a ditch after killing off my whole family. I was wounded. He's now at his house again. I saw him yesterday at the community office after he registered. I told him, "Behold, I am risen from the dead," and he replied, "It was a human hell," and he asked my pardon. He said, "It was the fault of the authorities who led us in these acts, seeking their own gains." He said he regretted it, and he asked my pardon.[11]

Nyirabeza said that no matter what Girumuhatse said, he was responsible for killing ten members of her family including her children and her grand-children. "[He] lives now with all his family and gets his property back, while I remain alone, without a child, without a husband."[12] She scoffed at the man's request for her pardon. "If he can bring back my children . . . and rebuild my house, maybe."[13]

Excellent journalist that he is, Gourevitch tracked down Girumuhatse and interviewed him:

He introduced himself as Jean Girumuhatse. I told him that his name was familiar to me because it was said in the community that he had killed a whole family. "It's true," Girumuhatse said. "They say I killed because I was the leader of the roadblock right here." He pointed to the road where it passed closest to his house. "Right now, all is well," he told me. "But then, at that time, we were called on by the state to kill. You were told you had the duty to do this or you'd be imprisoned or killed. We were just pawns in this. We were just tools."[14]

Hutus returning from the camps received a great deal of aid, while Tutsis who survived the genocide in Rwanda were given very little help. Hutus were reclaiming their houses, whereas Tutsis often had no houses left to reclaim. The families of exiled Tutsis who came to Rwanda often moved into uninhabited houses while surviving Tutsis families did with less, because it had not occurred to them to move in and claim the house of a former neighbor.

Peaceful Coexistence

When Paul Kagame was asked how he could expect survivors to live next to people who had killed, he said, "You don't necessarily just go for everyone you might think you should go for . . . Maybe you create an atmosphere where things are stabilized first, then you go for those you must go for. Others you can even ignore for the sake of gradually leading a kind of peaceful coexistence."[15]

Kagame knew he was asking a lot, and there were reports of soldiers rescuing alleged killers from angry mobs and placing them in "protective custody."[16] Sometimes people on each side killed or were killed. When Gourevitch asked him whether he still believed that killers could be successfully reintegrated into society, Kagame replied:

> I think you can't give up on that—on such a person . . . They can learn. I'm sure that every individual, somewhere in his plans, wants some peace, wants to progress in some way, even if he is an ordinary peasant. So if we can present the past to them and say, "This was the past that caused all these problems for you, and this is the way to avoid that," I think it changes their minds quite a bit. And I think some people can even benefit from being forgiven, being given another chance . . . We have no alternative.[17]

In the case of Jean Girumuhatse, at least, there were indications that this might be true. Gourevitch reported:

> As soon as he told me he was a killer, he stopped sweating. His breath came more easily. His eyes even looked clearer, and he seemed eager to keep talking.

A storm had blown in, dumping rain, so we moved into my jeep, which was parked right where Girumuhatse's roadblock had stood during the genocide. As we settled in, he announced that one reason he had been under pressure during the genocide was that he had been told to kill his wife, a Tutsi. "I was able to save my wife because I was the leader," he said, adding that he had feared for his own life, too. "I had to do it or I'd be killed," he said. "So I feel a bit innocent. Killing didn't come from my heart. If it was really my wish to kill, I couldn't now come back." [18]

Placing Blame

Girumuhatsi blamed Jean Paul Akayesu, the former mayor of Taba, for pushing him to kill. It was Akayesu who made Girumuhatsi the leader of the roadblock. Akayesu was an eager killer of Tutsis, who was arrested in Zambia in 1995 and convicted of genocide by the International Tribunal for Rwanda in 1998. Akayesu also became the first person in history found guilty of using rape as genocide because of his strategic use of the rape of 250,000 Tutsi women. Like the Nazis tried at Nuremberg, Akayesu blamed his political superiors for the killings. And so it went, with everyone blaming the people who were a step up from them, giving the orders.

When it got to the top, the people who organized the genocide attempted to blame it on the RPF, saying that if Kagame had not attacked the country, the genocide wouldn't have happened. They were saying, "We killed, because they attacked us." But that is not logical reasoning. The RPF attack was an invasion from outside of the country. Just because they were led by Tutsis didn't justify murdering Tutsis who were members of your society and living in the country.

Why kill them? Why kill a baby? Why rape a young girl? Why kill an old woman? They were never part of the RPF. Why shoot a baby on the lap of its mother? Because the RPF has attacked? This argument never really made sense. The perpetrators of the genocide used this as an excuse, because they didn't have anything else to say. There is no justification for genocide.

The evil of the genocide in Rwanda was so great that no one can find any form of rational justification for it. The best explanations are closer to what Girumuhatse told Philip Gourevitch after admitting his involvement. The genocide "was like a dream," he said. "It came from the regime like a nightmare."[19]

Longing for "Before"

The internal confusion and strife continued throughout most of 1997. The people were unhappy, and they were poor. France had provided the lion's share of foreign aid to Rwanda in the days before the genocide. For a year after the government fell, they did not provide any money, and Rwanda began establishing a taxation program to survive. Soon, other countries gradually began to help, and eventually France joined them in some ways. The first few years were very hard, however, and this only added to the people's discontent.

The truth is that the people of Rwanda wanted the impossible. They wanted to go back in time. It was common to hear people talk and use the word *before* without any further explanation. "Before" meant before the genocide, when life was good, before the pain, before the anger, before the loss. Most of the survivors at that time were merely existing. They'd lost family members and friends in horrible ways. Very few had the faith to have much hope in the future. And as long as this state of mind existed, there was a very real danger of some sort of mass slaughter returning.

The Miracle of Forgiveness

If someone told these people to kill their neighbors because they killed your families, a great many of them would have done it, because they did not believe in the future anyway. People who have seen their sisters raped and their brothers chopped to death do not easily forgive and forget. It requires a miracle just to get them to try.

When I was coming in from Uganda to hold the conferences, there was a lot of fear. People were afraid to have a Tutsi sit close to a Hutu, and even if they sat together, they wouldn't look at each other or feel comfortable—smiling and talking together as they used to, before the genocide. That agitation soon faded, and the problem became not one of possible violent engagement as much as one of suspicion, guilt, and fear of retaliation.

When I began announcing programs for healing and forgiveness, some people criticized me for not moving on. But this is not something you can simply move on from without divine help. You don't forget the brutal murders of your loved ones. It is not even our mission to tell people to forget, but only to forgive with God's help. And you certainly can't forgive yourself for killing innocent people. God has to be a part of that.

This was the challenge I faced after I returned to Rwanda. But I knew that God had set my life for His service and His ministry in this situation. This was my home country. God had a purpose for my country and a purpose for me. I knew that the perpetrators of the genocide were suffering from the worst guilt any human society has ever suffered through, and I knew personally the incredible pain the victims of the genocide suffered. God made it clear to me that both sides needed a divine intervention to rescue them. God wanted to touch them.

I knew that to really minister to Rwanda's needs meant working toward reconciliation in the prisons, in the churches, and in the cities and villages throughout the country. It meant feeding the hungry, sheltering the homeless, caring for the young, but it also meant healing the wounded and forgiving the unforgivable.

I knew I had to be committed to preaching a transforming message to the people of Rwanda. Jesus did not die for people to be religious. He died so that we might believe in Him and be transformed. I'm engaged in a purpose and strategy that Jesus came to Earth for. My life is set for that divine purpose in Jesus Christ. I was called to that—proclaiming the message of transformation through Jesus Christ.

NINE

Uncovering the Truth

Arusha Courts

In November 1994, the United Nations established an international tribunal to oversee prosecution of the perpetrators of the genocide. In an effort to unite the country, the new Rwandan government ordered a moratorium on arrests of those suspected of involvement. In December 1996, the UN tribunal in Arusha began trying some of the organizers and well-known perpetrators of the genocide; by January 10, 1997, three former Hutu Power advocates were convicted and sentenced to death.

Of course there were reprisals and resistance. In mid-January, a woman who had testified against Jean Paul Akayesu was murdered—along with her husband and seven children—by Hutu extremists. A week later, when the Rwandan army tried to capture Hutu insurgents who were responsible for killing many recently returned refugees who were potential trial witnesses, as well as three Spanish aid workers in northwestern Rwanda, three hundred people were killed. Then on February 2, Hutu terrorists murdered Canadian priest Guy Pinard, a witness to the genocide, while he said mass.

This was a time when violent people still thought they could use their violence to get their way. Not all the deaths were related to the genocide. On

February 4, five human rights observers were killed in an ambush near Cysngugu by Hutu terrorists who wanted foreign observers to leave the country. The UN then withdrew all their observers in Kibuye and Hisenyi to Kigali, where they could better protect them.

On Valentine's Day, 1997, Vincent Nkezabaganwa, a Rwandan supreme court justice, was gunned down by uniformed gunmen at his house. That same day, Frodouard Karamira, leader of a Hutu extremist political movement, was sentenced to death for his involvement in the genocide. Karamira had coined the slogan "Hutu Power" and frequently urged mass murder during his racist radio broadcasts. He expressed no remorse for the part he played in the genocide. In a classic touch of irony, many people said Karamira was actually born a Tutsi, but presented himself as a Hutu for most of his life.

Slow Progress in Arusha

It wasn't long before people realized that the International Court of Justice in Arusha was not really performing according to the expectations of the people. Very little was getting accomplished. By the end of 1999, they had only tried and convicted six people. Six people in three years! Investigations were conducted and several problems discovered. First of all, some people involved in the genocide had changed their identities and were working in Arusha—people who should have been on trial were actually part of the justice process.

After these people were discovered, there were some demonstrations, and the people in question were dismissed. Then it was discovered that the head of the tribunal was not objective. She was sympathetic to the Hutu Power forces and not for a peaceful Rwanda. These were some of the reasons the process was so slow. To make matters worse, the Arusha courts took billions of dollars from the UN.

Eventually, other discrepancies were discovered. Many witnessses reported they had been pressured in Arusha. They were asked things like, "Okay, you say you were raped. How did they do it? Tell us step-by-step what happened and how it made you feel." It was dehumanizing, and people began refusing to go to Arusha to bear witness. There were demonstrations, and Rwanda was on the verge of officially boycotting the courts.

Arrests

At this time most of the key players in the genocide were hiding in other African nations. In July, Paul Kagame visited Kenya's aging strongman, Daniel arap Moi, who had broken off relations with Rwanda following the genocide. Two days later, seven of the most-wanted masterminds of the genocide were arrested and turned over to the UN tribunal at Arusha. Though Moi had been their friend, he now denounced them as "foreign spies and criminals."[1]

The arrests included RGF General Gratien Kabiligi, who had recently commanded the Hutu Power forces in the Congo; Georges Ruggiu, the broadcaster for radio RTLM; and Hassan Ngeze, who published the Hutu Ten Commandments and forecast President Habyarimana's death in the newspaper *Kangura*.

The two most prominent arrests were of Théoneste Bagosora, who led the government after President Habyarimana's assassination and whom prosecutors believe was the chief architect of the genocide; and Jean Kambanda, who became prime minister after the assassination of Madame Agathe Uwilingiyimana. Kambanda—a leading member of the radical Hutu party, the *Mouvement Democratique Populaire*—fled to the Congo and later Kenya, where he was arrested in Nairobi and extradited to the tribunal in neighboring Tanzania. He confessed and received a sentence of life imprisonment.

Bagosora was arrested on March 9, 1996, in Yaounde (Cameroon) and transferred to the United Nations prison quarters in Arusha on January 23, 1997. His trial began on April 2, 2002, and he pleaded not guilty. As of this writing, Bagosora's trial continues after a year of testimony. Information that surfaced during the trial included that, on the morning of April 7, 1994, Bagosora is said to have personally given the order to the Interahamwe to begin the extermination of the Tutsi civilian population.

On the same day he reportedly ordered Major Ntabakuze, Major Nzuwonemeye, and Lieutenant Colonel Nkundiye to start the massacres.

That day radio channels broadcast a message from Bagosora, asking the population to stay home and await further instructions after Habyarimana's assassination, an act that simplified the murder of Tutsis and moderate Hutus across the country.

Other prominent figures in the genocide who are imprisoned and still on trial in Arusha are Jerome Bicamumpaka, former minister of foreign affairs; Casimir Bizimungu, former minister of health; Edouard Karemera, former minister of interior for the interim government and vice president of the MRND political party; Justin Mugenzi, former minister of commerce; Prosper Mugiraneza, former minister of civil service; Mathieu Ngirumpatse, former director general of the ministry for foreign affairs and president of the MRND; Pauline Nyiramasuhuko, former minister of family and women affairs; Joseph Nzirorera, former president of the national assembly and secretary general of the MRND; Andre Rwamakuba, former minister of education; and Augustin Bizimungu, former chief of staff of the Rwandan Army.

Pauline Nyiramasuhuko's case drew worldwide attention because she is the first woman in history to be charged with crimes against humanity and, in yet another horrible Rwandan irony, the woman once in charge of the well-being of Rwanda's women, is also charged with rape as genocide.

Twenty-six people have been executed, but more than four hundred have received the death sentence.[2] Eventually, 125,000 people were arrested and put in jail for their involvement in the genocide. That is a very small portion of the people who actually participated, but President Kagame has tried to focus on the planners and organizers rather than perpetrators. When you consider that a nation of only 8,000,000 people hacked to death 1,117,000 of those people in only a hundred days, it becomes clear that there was mass participation.

There were many Hutu who didn't kill, many who saved people, and even some who died trying. There were entire villages wiped out where no one was left to give testimony. Most of the people arrested were either caught in the act, or there were witnesses who testified against them. There are also countless numbers in the villages who participated in one way or another without actually killing anyone—by pointing out those who were supposed to be killed, by revealing hiding places, or by ignoring the situation and doing nothing to stop the slaughter.

Still at Large

All the participators could not be prosecuted; there would be no country left. Many of the people who should have been prosecuted, the actual designers and masterminds of the genocide, are still outside of the country. Many are in France, Belgium, or other parts of Europe. Many are hiding in America and elsewhere. They exploited and looted the nation, so most of them have a great deal of money.

Reconciliation in Action

Bringing the guilty to justice is one thing, but healing the guilt is another. Most everyone who participated in the genocide has a great degree of guilt inside. Ironically, those who were the least guilty sometimes have the greatest guilt because they knew it was wrong and did it anyway. Absolving the peasants of guilt, because in many cases they were manipulated or even forced to participate in the killing, may stop them from going to jail, but it will not stop them from feeling the guilt.

Denial

This is where my role comes in. The people who work with me in this ministry and I are not only working toward healing the anger of the victimized, but also toward healing the guilt of those who participated. Denial is, of course, a key issue. All over the world today, people go to great extremes to avoid pain, but the reality is that pain is already there. People want to move on and put something as terrible as the genocide behind them, but they cannot move on until they deal with this inner guilt.

When people are in denial or trying to cover up their actions, their guilt becomes even greater. It begins to eat away at them like acid, and they start to die from within. That is why our calling is so important. We have to get involved in the community and reach people. In Rwanda, that is more than a matter of using the media. We have to reach the people where they are, in the remote villages as well as in the cities, and so we hold conferences in these communities.

Awash with Guilt—The Walking Dead

The local government helps us. The head of each district helps us organize the pastors and the churches to reach the people in the villages near a conference, and a great many usually attend. We bring a message of healing and reconciliation. We have lost a million people, and we don't want to lose another three million because of the guilt. Much of Rwanda is awash with guilt. So many are overcome by it that they are like the walking dead.

In most cases they have been afraid to reveal their guilt. They were coming into churches with guilt, and they were going out with guilt. I asked the Lord to give me a comprehensive ministry and realized that healing the wounded from the scars of the genocide also meant healing those with guilt. I began preaching reconciliation between Hutus and Tutsis, which is the reconciliation of Rwanda.

God gave me the courage to tell the community that the guilt of the genocide is not only for those who can be arrested, but also for all the guilty. At the same time, many who were innocent have felt unnecessary guilt because their kinsmen were involved. We had to encourage them to be free and proclaim their innocence. There is no reason why people should feel guilty because they were members of the same family or, for that matter, the same ethnic group. That was what was wrong with the Hutu Power philosophy in the first place—it tried to condemn an entire ethnic group because of the perceived injustices of a few.

That's why it's very important for me to make known that there were many Hutus who suffered during the genocide. There were many who took risks to save Tutsis. In fact, a Hutu rescued almost every Tutsi who was saved, and there were many Hutus who died trying to do right.

Emphasis on Similarities

The key to reconciliation is to find where you come together—what unites you—your common source. Many clans of Tutsis and clans of Hutus have discovered that they come from the same clan. Some called themselves Hutus, and others called themselves Tutsis. My father and my uncle used to tell me that there were some Hutus in our family line. Every year many Tutsis and Hutus go to a shrine traditional in their family lines. At a lot of these shrines, both Hutus and Tutsis come to make a yearly sacrifice to honor their ancestors. Obviously they have a common source in their family line. Why should we emphasize our differences and promote violence when we can emphasize our similarities and promote peace?

When I was young, there was a problem between the southern people and the northern people of Rwanda. The southerners were called *Abayendoda*, and the northern people were called *Abarella*. There were Tutsis and Hutus among both groups. The division was between north and south, not Hutu and Tutsi. The point is the devil is always trying to divide us, and he will always come up with reasons for division.

When we talk about unity and reconciliation and Rwanda, we are not just talking about reconciliation between Hutu and Tutsi. There are other divisions that could destroy our country as well. Some of us are Christian. Some of us are Muslim. A very few are rich. A great many are poor. Some are well educated. Some are illiterate. We must look at our similarities and not let our differences divide us.

The Bible says God created us in His own image. It couldn't have been talking about our skin, because our skins are so different. The image of God is not in the outside appearance, but inside. It's in our minds and in our hearts. To have reconciliation in Rwanda, we must try hard to tune in to that image of God inside us. During the genocide, beautiful Hutu women were often killed because they were assumed to be Tutsis just because they were beautiful. It's not what is on the outside that matters, but what is on the inside.

And life on the inside is the real life—do we have peace, do we love, do we do right by others, are we seeking God? Jesus said, "I am the door of the sheep.

. . . If anyone enters by Me, he will be saved, and will go in and out and find pasture. The theif does not come except to steal, and to kill, and to destroy. I have come that they may have life, and that they may have it more abundantly" (John 10:7–10 NKJV).

Rwanda Is Crying

Jesus came so that we may have life and have it abundantly. I ask the people in our reconciliation meetings if they feel they have abundant life. And most of them will say no. They can't deny it. They don't have abundant life. They aren't happy. I call upon everyone in this country to cry out—ministers, mayors—take your microphones, speak louder, and tell people that Rwanda is crying. She wants to be healed!

People who have not experienced God's forgiveness in a spiritual sense have a hard time understanding the kind of reconciliation we are experiencing in Rwanda, and many of those people speak against me. They say, "Bishop John, why do you go to share with the people who did the genocide?" But I have to go there, because those people also need to know the Lord and be made well so they can become good citizens and join others to develop a new Rwanda.

Of course, just as the perpetrators are afraid they will be punished, the survivors are afraid they will be hurt again. Some people feel it's better to leave things alone, because engaging it causes pain. I remember getting a telephone call from a group of young soldiers when I announced my plan to reconcile prisoners with the survivors of the genocide. These young men called and said, "Bishop John, it looks as though your program is about helping these criminals, these killers, these evil men who hacked a million people to death. Not only are you trying to get them set free, but you are working to bless them with salvation and intending to take them to heaven before the victims."

And I replied, "That is true. We want them to repent, ask forgiveness, and reconcile to their victims. And then they will be able to not only go to heaven, but to have peace here before they die." They were upset, and it's not easy for a cleric to have such a conversation with a group of soldiers. They want the men in prison to suffer, but I know I was called by God to help them get healed.

At the reconciliation meetings I ask if anyone has forgotten what they were doing during the genocide. Everyone remembers. Who can forget such an experience? But the really important question is, who are they now? Has the horror of the genocide so scarred them that they have not recovered? It is hard for someone to conceive of that much personal pain disappearing, but somehow God can take away the pain, even while He leaves the memory. But they have to allow Him to come into their hearts.

A man in one of our reconciliation meetings stood up and said, "Before confessing my sins, I couldn't sleep, because if I dreamed, I might dream about what I did during the genocide. And that thought, that voice that says 'You're wrong' all the time was loud in my head. You can't forget what you did. It continues to tear at your heart. But since I asked forgiveness for my sins, I have been able to sleep."

Igihong

I am calling the people of Rwanda not to harm or betray anyone, and to ask forgiveness from those whom they have harmed or betrayed. There is something we call *Igihong*. In one of our traditional ways of creating intimacy or fellowship, people make a small cut on their thumb and then drink each other's blood as a bond of our fellowship. The idea is that if I later disappoint you as a friend, that blood will follow me with a curse. My children can even suffer for it. So if we don't come to the Lord and ask Him to heal us, we are going to be cursed. But if we have courage and speak up about what we did, if we say, "I killed this person," or "I hated my brother," God will heal us and bless us.

We have to work for healing in Rwanda. And that includes healing the damage that the churches did to the people. In the conferences I ask the people, "Who poisoned us?" And one time a man raised his hand and said, "Bishop, the church leaders are the ones who poisoned us." And I said, "Yes, you are right. Who else poisoned us?" And then someone said, "The government at the time of the genocide poisoned us and also the colonialists." And he is right also.

I tell them, "The church leaders didn't speak the truth. The politicians didn't speak the truth. I repent on behalf of my brothers and sisters who were church leaders before and during the genocide. Many of us poisoned you, and for that I am deeply sorry." But now the people must accept that those who gave them poison want them to vomit it out so they may be healed. They need to vomit out the memory of that experience—vomit out the problems in their hearts.

We want God to bless them, to give them peace in their hearts, to give them the strength to stand up and witness and work for the development of this country. When a person is angry, he becomes bitter. And bitterness can eat at you like acid. If you don't repent of it, you become scarred forever. We have to repent of our sins, our hatred. When God finished creating the mountains of Rwanda, He said, "This is really beautiful." And that is how it was meant to be.

There is a good song that says: "The crowns are prepared for everybody who will reach heaven." But you won't get to have such a crown if you still hate your neighbor. No Umahutu will get that crown when he or she hates Umatutsi. No Umatutsi will get that divine crown when he or she hates Umahutu. It is not easy to let go of hatred, but it is worth it for that crown. God gave us life here in this world, but also He's preparing eternal life in heaven. And life in heaven is not only greater than the life here on earth, but the life in this world is short, and the life in heaven is forever. The pain of this life, even in Rwanda, is nothing compared to the joy that awaits those who choose heaven.

Stages of Reconciliation

Not everyone can heal at the same rate. People go through different stages. We are talking about extreme emotional pain in Rwanda. In the early stages many people are not even able to discuss what happened to them during the genocide. They can't bear to think about it, much less talk about it on a conscious level. But on a subconscious level, it is probably all they think about.

We have to go slowly with these people. Otherwise they break into pieces immediately and run away. They need more time to heal before they can trust God enough to ask Him to help them to forgive. There are a lot of tears involved, and it is only with God's help that any progress can be made. You have to depend on God, and you have to go little by little.

For example, we move from a large conference that discusses the importance of getting healed, to a small conference for genocide survivors that maybe has only ten or twenty people. Then we try to get people to share. It is sometimes easier to share in a group if it is not too large, but you have to give them time to shed tears, to release emotions that they may be bottling up. Of course, we cry as well. Sometimes you can't help it when they share the horrors they experienced. You wind up joining them in tears.

The woman who told us about her sister's baby being killed on her lap, two years ago, could not even talk about what happened to her family. It has been a long journey to reach where she is today. She's been through several conferences and several counseling sessions. She now has a general forgiveness for Hutus.

But she would not be comfortable around the people she knows killed the members of her family. She certainly would not be able to eat with them or have them come into her house. Two years from today she might be able to talk to a group of people in public about it, giving her name and even letting someone take her picture. But that is still a long way away for her.

There are some people who can speak more freely. There are many who have forgiven those who murdered their family, and these people are the freest of all. You can see it. We have some people who have already forgiven to the extent that they are able to live, work, and eat with those they have forgiven.

This is an ongoing mission. This ministry requires persistence and commitment. We want to unearth the realities. And once we do that, we have to help the people process those realities, and that takes time. Revenge is like a disease that eats away at us from the inside. We therefore have to forgive in order to live. Forgiveness not only helps the perpetrators of the genocide, but it also helps the victims. It works both ways. When we forgive, we get healed.

Reconciliation Among Church Leaders

There also has been reconciliation between the churches. Many denominations work together in the prison ministry, and others are working on healing the scars from the genocide. Until recently there has not been a relationship between Anglican clergy and Catholic clergy, but now we are working together. This bothers some people, because they have a hard time accepting anything different from what they're used to.

Even Jesus had to rebuke people for thinking that way. John the Baptist came without eating, without drinking wine, and they said he was under a demon's power. Then when Jesus came drinking and eating, they said he was a drunkard and a glutton. When the churches couldn't work together, people said it wasn't right, and now that we are working together, people worry that something is wrong.

The cooperation between Christian leaders has not only crossed denominational lines, but also attracted prominent evangelicals, like Joyce Meyer and Rick Warren. Joyce Meyer held a crusade in Rwanda in April 2006. Her ministries have built two houses in Kigali for genocide survivors and minister in the prisons as well.

Rick Warren and his wife, Kay, are very good friends to Rwanda. Rick's "business in a box" plan, for example, helps villagers grow beyond subsistence living. Rick updated the idea that "If you give people fish, you feed them for a day, but if you teach them how to fish, you feed them for a lifetime" and added that if you teach someone how to sell the fish they catch, you can affect the economy of an entire country. He is helping Rwandans learn sales and marketing skills.

When President Kagame read *The Purpose Driven Life*, he wrote to author Rick Warren, saying, "I am a purpose-driven man." He invited Warren and others to Kigali. In March 2006, Rick and Kay Warren, some of the leaders from Rick's Saddleback Church, a few business leaders, and William Beasley met with several of us—Rwandan Anglican bishops and some of Rwanda's political leaders. "I fell in love with the country," Warren said. "I prayed, 'Lord, help me find out what You are blessing and help me get in on it.' I think God is blessing Rwanda."

God at Work

You know God is doing something when people in different places begin to have the same ideas even before they are connected. It's not just our idea.

It's our vision. We held a crusade at the stadium when Rick and the others were here. It was based on Rick's Peace Project. The mission of the project is for Rwandans to be productive and actively working on issues of health and education, encouraging people to produce, empowering leadership, and most important, having a relationship with Jesus Christ.

During the crusade we had a genocide perpetrator and a survivor witnessing on the same platform. They have a heavy burden and were shedding a lot of tears. They became friends and now travel together, giving their witness. That's how reconciliation works.

Rick is now encouraging teams of people from his church to come to different communities in Rwanda so they can help the people perform their best in different fields and on different levels.

My friend William Beasley is an Anglican pastor under PEER *(Province Eglise Episcopale au Rwanda),* from the Chicago area. He has been working with Rwanda since 1998. He, too, sees leaders bringing together their resources in new ways to help the country. Beasley said, "A country that was abandoned by the world has been adopted by the church."

New Policies and New Attitudes

The identification cards and passports for Rwandan citizens just say "Rwanda" now, without any reference to whether the person is Hutu or Tutsi, because that type of classification was applied for evil and destruction. That may sound like a simple step, but it removes the ability to determine a person's ethnic group, because most people reflect the blend of the two groups that is our history. You cannot persecute or even resent what you can't identify.

America made a nation with people from all over Europe. Here we are in Rwanda, looking pretty much the same, with one language and one culture, and yet we have failed to become a nation until now, because someone from Europe told us we should be separate. We are not separate. We are intermingled in society everywhere—in churches, in jobs, in offices. We are together.

A hundred years ago there might have been many more pure Tutsis or Hutus, but now that is rarely the case. That is one of the things that made the genocide so ludicrous. For centuries, no one gave any thought to Hutus and Tutsis marrying each other. Then it became a taboo for some, but all that is disappearing again. Since we all live and work together, they couldn't stop men and women from falling in love and marrying and having children together. Love is not limited by social guidelines.

Our government is doing everything possible to bring about reconciliation. Persecution is not allowed, and neither is revenge. But while these policies can bring calmness to the community—an outer peace, if you will—attaining inner peace requires something more. The wounds and the guilt must be healed. Our challenge is to engage the gospel and promote honest communication and healing so that there can be inner peace as well.

The country also has been rebuilt in the physical sense. After the genocide the new government organized community workdays, where people were encouraged to volunteer for public service—building roads, turning vacant lots into brickyards from which new homes could be built for the displaced citizens, etc. Philip Gourevitch recalled seeing Paul Kagame working at one site, spading mud into a wooden brick frame, among a crowd of ragged laborers:

> "This is soldier's work, too," [Kagame] told me. A few feet away, a man was down on his knees, swinging a big machete, chopping up straw to mix into the mud. He had just come back from Zaire, and he said he was rather astonished, after hearing "Monsieur le Vice-President" demonized in the camps, to see him there. "But it's normal," he added, "because every authority who wants to work for the country must set the example for the people." [3]

Rwanda has to move away from its hatred and pain. Only then can we realize true freedom and make the country what it should be. We have to develop ourselves before we can develop the country. That means more than just wearing shoes and having cars. It means having a good diet, building strong houses, and teaching our children. But to do that, we have to work together and be freed from the horrors of our past.

To be freed we have to open ourselves up to the Lord so He can heal us and in the process heal our country. "If My people who are called by My name will humble themselves, and pray and seek My face, and turn from their wicked ways, then I will hear from heaven, and will forgive their sin and heal their land" (2 Chronicles 7:14 NKJV).

Changing Hearts

Prison Ministry

By the end of 1997, Rwandan jails were bursting at the seams, holding 125,000 people arrested for crimes committed during the genocide. I knew that God wanted me to reach these people for Him, and ultimately to heal the nation, but it seemed an awesome task.

The first thing we did was to hold a national conference on reconciliation. We involved the government people—the minister of internal affairs, the minister of security, and others. I began to recruit people to help me. One of the first was Deo Gashagaza, who today is the director of the prison ministry. Deo recalled: "We met with people from Prison Fellowship International and discussed their approach. We liked what they had to say because it centered around the gospel. Then we applied to the government so that our organization could go into the prisons and meet with the men. When we obtained permission, we organized a small group and began visiting the prisons."

We then held a conference for all the prison directors, the prison social workers, people from Ebuka (an organization of survivors of the genocide) and Avega (an organization for widows of the genocide), and many other involved people. We organized volunteers to work in prisons throughout the country to bring a message of salvation, repentance, forgiveness, and reconcil-iation. The results proved very effective.

"God opened many doors for us, and the prison ministry grew very fast," Deo said. "As soon as the government began to see the results, they began to help us more and more. They began to realize that we play an important role in the transformation of these people."

In some ways it's easier to reach people in the jails. Today's fast-paced life offers numerous escapes if we choose them. But when people are confined, their thoughts catch up to them, and they can't push them out by escaping into drugs, alcohol, or other things. When we preach in the prisons, people are open to hearing the message, and very often they end up in tears. Often, the director of the prison will tell us that it is the first time he has seen people in his jail cry.

It has not been that long ago. The prisoners still play the tapes of their vio-lence in their minds. They hear the voices of the people who were pleading for mercy. They see the drama of the people lifting their hands, asking for mercy, and still they continued cutting those arms off. I ask them, "Have you forgot-ten that?" And they say no and shake their heads as they cry.

I tell them that God is calling them to come to terms with their conscience. I remind them of the passage in Luke about the widow and the merciless judge. Then I say, "That merciless judge is your heart, because it never forgives you. It always plays the tape. It always gives you the sound of the voices of the people you killed. You were raised with them; you went to school with them; you know the sound of their voices.

"To silence those voices, you need to repent, honestly, and ask God to forgive you. That judge inside your heart, your conscience that judges you, will stop judging you only when you come to terms with God. And those videos will stop playing in your mind only when you truly repent and God forgives you.

"There are people on the street who might as well be in jail, because their hearts are imprisoned. They are in Paris or New York, all over the world, but they are not free. They are in jail as much as you are in jail. They cry as much as you cry. At night they see what you see. They are out of jail, and yet they continue to be in jail. The bars are in their hearts. Don't let that happen to you."

Most of the time, the people in the prisons are open to speaking the truth, confessing, and repenting. Sometimes they even upgrade their files and reveal the names of people they killed. After I preached at a certain prison, a gentleman said, "My file says I killed cows and looted property, but—God forgive me—I killed a family. We wiped out that family at night, and no one survived." So he went to the prosecutor and upgraded his file, because he wanted to put it right.

Living as Neighbors Again

Gradually, the entire nation of Rwanda has seemed to embrace repentance and forgiveness. The Rwandan parliament passed a national initiative allowing prisoners to apply for a pardon after they confessed their crimes. Prisoners who participated in the prison ministry benefited immediately from the program, and this became a powerful incentive for others. The prison ministry's new challenge was to develop a way to connect those in the jails with the genocide survivors in the communities they would be returning to when they were released.

I had been holding reconciliation conferences in many areas, so Deo and I met with some of the survivors of the genocide and sought their input about how to best integrate these men back into the community. Most of these people grew up in the same area that their ancestors were from, and the vast majority of them will return to that same area when they are released from prison. That means that the survivors and perpetrators are going to have to learn to live together as neighbors again.

"How Can I Ask for Forgiveness?"

To be considered for the pardon program requires confession and asking for forgiveness. Most have done the first step, but many struggle with the second. "How can I ask for forgiveness," asked a prisoner in Ruhengeri, "when there were so many who begged me for mercy during the genocide, and I ignored them?"

African culture is such that these men are very concerned about the honor or dishonor they have brought their ancestors. A prisoner here does not confess and ask forgiveness just so he or she can get out of prison. It goes much deeper than that. It is often difficult for people to accept forgiveness, and this is something people need to be taught.

"There are some prisoners who, when we started working with them, were traumatized by what they had done," Deo said. "And after they accepted Christ and went through confession and asking for forgiveness, they were healed. And then the word spread about this throughout the prison, and more people were drawn to the program."

Transformation Transcends Denominations

The biggest problem the Prison Fellowship faces is obtaining the people and funds necessary to take the message everywhere that it needs to be heard. The program also teaches prisoners to read and write. Most of the financing comes from the many churches that support it.

"The Prison Fellowship is a ministry composed of many denominations," Deo said. "Bishop John is Anglican, and his partner in the fellowship is Roman Catholic. I'm from a Baptist church. The message we are preaching transcends denominational differences."

The message seems to reach people all across the board, from villagers who just went along with the government program to the former army and Interahamwe militia.

"The power of the gospel comes through," Deo believes, "whether a person was an avid organizer who wanted the genocide or someone who just got caught up in it. It reaches everyone, and it changes their hearts."

We don't preach religion when we go to the prisons. We simply tell them the gospel. We are coming to tell them the Word of Life, the Good News of Jesus Christ, how the Word of God tells them their relationship with God can be restored, and that it will restore their life as a person. We don't say, "Come and be Anglicans." We say, "Come and be alive in Jesus Christ and in the presence of God." We are preaching the transformation of lives.

The archbishop above me in the Anglican Church is also a member of the Prison Fellowship. He's very supportive. The church never pressures me to make Anglican converts because they know who I am and what God has called me to do. And they know that many people are suspicious of the clergy. Many prisoners want to know why the clergy didn't try to stop them from killing people. These people know when you are sincere.

Preparation for Life on the Outside

Part of the work of the prison ministry is preparing people for life on the outside. This includes the possibility of being confronted with dramatic changes from the time they were arrested. I tell them, "Some of you are going to find that your wives have committed adultery. They may even have children who are not yours. What are you going to do? Are you going to kill them? Some of you will find your wives have sold your land. But perhaps they sold your land because they wanted to bring food to you while you were still here in prison. Are you going to kill them?"

They need to prepare themselves to deal with difficult situations. I tell them a story about a man who was released from prison and bought some biscuits to take to his children. When he arrived at his home, he found that his wife had another child. He handed out the biscuits to his children, and then his youngest son said, "Papa, why haven't you given biscuits to that child?"

He said, "Who is that child?"

And the boy said, "It's the child of my mother."

Then the father said, "No, I don't know him." And he became very bitter, but the boy was right. It was the child of his mother, and if the family was to go on, the father had to embrace that.

There are people who pretend they are innocent in order to be released, but if they are deceptive and haven't repented of their guilt, they will commit more crimes after they are free. I tell them about a man who was released from jail and killed his four children. When this man was freed, he didn't go straight home. He met a very beautiful lady and fell in love with her. He told the woman that he wanted to sleep with her and marry her.

But the lady said, "I know that you have a wife. How can you get married to me? You have a wife and four children."

The man said, "Don't worry. I know what to do. I have my panga. I'm going to cut the neck of my former wife, and I will even kill my children."

And he did. He strangled his children and tried to kill his wife with a machete so that he could marry the lady he had met. The wife cried out, and people came and rescued her.

I tell the men in prison that it was the curse of the man's hatred that caused him to kill his children. If you don't want to remove the problems that are between you and your neighbors, the curse will come down to your children. Holding on to anger is not something that ends even when you die. Instead it gets passed on to your children. By remaining angry, you train them to be angry as well.

You can't cover this up. Your children will know. They will ask, "Papa, why is that blanket there?" And if you don't tell them that you're covering something up, they will uncover it themselves. You have to be truthful so that you can pass on truth to your children. If you lie, you will pass on those lies to your children, and your children will pass them on to your grandchildren.

We don't want this genocidal pain and guilt passed on to the next generation. It is better for us to suffer a little more now, so that we can heal this suffering once and for all. Then we can pass the healing on to the next generation.

I feel very strongly that God has called me to actively preach in the prisons, to love these men and women, to pray for their honest repentance and a turnabout in their lives. It must come from the heart, from the inside out, and that means God has to move them to receive it. I tell my pastors, "You can't expect the people to trust you because of your collars or your uniforms. That trust was forsaken during the genocide. Now they will only trust you after you prove who you are. It is by your character and your teaching that they will learn to trust you."

Government Involvement in Reconciliation

Most of what we are doing could not be done without the help of the Rwandan government. President Kagame has been a leader in the reconciliation process from the moment he took office and announced that the exiles, both Hutu and Tutsi, were welcome back to Rwanda. He put a moratorium on arrests, he advocated the community courts, he initiated the process that freed those who were underage when they committed their crimes, and he helped establish the program where prisoners who confess, repent, and ask forgiveness can be freed.

The government has also done other things that help the reconciliation process, such as changing the national flag. The former Rwandan flag had become a symbol of hatred and division. It was red and green, and the Hutu Power advocates claimed that the red was for the blood of Hutus who were killed by Tutsis during the colonial days, and the green symbolized Hutu prosperity. Besides the flag, the national anthem was also changed for the same reasons. It was divisive. The new flag and the new national anthem celebrate our togetherness as one people, instead of emphasizing the differences.

Reconciliation Programs

The Umuvumu Tree Project. Prison Fellowship International developed the Sycamore Tree Project. It brings prisoners and victims together over a period of eight meetings to discuss what the Bible says about responsibility, confession, forgiveness, repentance, reconciliation, and restitution.

Its name was taken from the biblical account of Zacchaeus, the tax collector, who climbed the sycamore tree to get a better look at Jesus. When Jesus came to his house that day to dine, Zacchaeus repented of his sins and tried to make restitution to the people he had wronged. We have adapted the program for use in Rwanda, and we call our program the Umuvumu Tree Project, because that's the tree we have in our country that is closest to the sycamore tree. If Zacchaeus had met Jesus in Kigali instead of Jericho, the umuvumu is the tree he would have climbed.

Developed with the help of Prison Fellowship International's Dan Van Ness and Peter Walker, the Umuvumu Tree Project includes six weeks of small-group discussion among the prisoners, followed by two weeks of presentations by genocide survivors and prisoners' family members. Although the government made it an official policy to give lighter sentences to those who confessed their crimes, only five thousand prisoners had done so when the Umuvumu Tree Project began in mid-2002. Less than six months later, more than thirty-two thousand prisoners had confessed, and many of them had accepted Christ into their lives.

Nemeye Saveri was a farmer in Mbyo (Gashora District) before the genocide. He admitted to killing seven people.

In prison, my heart was broken. I felt the graveness of the sin I had committed. I read the Bible, which showed me how sinful I was. The government led us to believe that what we were doing was right and in the interest of the nation, but the Prison Fellowship members taught us that it was wrong and we needed to repent and ask for forgiveness from God and those we wronged. I feared revenge from those whose loved ones we killed, but the Umuvumu Tree Project helped us and those we wronged to meet through Christian teachings. I thank the genocide survivors for forgiving us. We reached a point when we hugged each other. That miracle was only possible because of our inward convictions that came from the teachings we received.

Another ex-prisoner who spoke about the benefits of the Umuvumu Tree Project was Ndaguza Ignace.

I was also a farmer, but I used to be a soldier, and when the genocide began, I was recalled. I was given a gun, and I took part in the genocide. I admitted that I took part, and I was arrested and sentenced to thirteen years' imprisonment. When the decree was passed to release all prisoners who had denounced what they had done during the genocide, I was released because I had repented and accepted what I had done. Now I live in the same village with people who lost their loved ones. It was only through God and the teachings I received through the Umuvumu project and the Prison Fellowship that I got the strength to ask for forgiveness and was able to live with those whose relatives had been killed in the genocide.

Change to Change. Another very important reconciliation program is called Change to Change and is based on the Acts of the Apostles and Others. On the day of Pentecost, people had come to Jerusalem from all over the world—Egypt, Cappadocia, Alexandria, Asia—and then the Spirit came, and Peter preached to them. Afterward the people asked, "After hearing all of this, what do we do?" And Peter and the apostles said, "Repent, because the promise of God in Jesus Christ is for you and for your children."

So they repented and went back home, and they changed their communities, because they had witnessed that outpouring of the Holy Spirit. They went home preaching and sharing the gospel. It's like the woman at the well in Samaria. After she met Jesus, she went to the people in the town and said, "I've seen a prophet, a man who knew all that has happened in my life. Come and see." She was used by God to invite others to meet Jesus. And when they met Jesus, they told her, "We have seen it. We have seen Him, and we have believed. Not because you told us, but because we have met Him too."

That's the process—people changing in order to be used by God to change others. God saved them for a purpose, to save other people. This is part of our strategic plan to reconcile people in this country: first, to reconcile them with God and their consciences, and then to reconcile them with others.

While those who have asked forgiveness and those who have forgiven may still be a smaller number than those who have not, they are very vocal about the peace this has given them, and they are very effective in sharing this peace. They have a confidence, an independence, a freedom that is empowerment from the Holy Spirit, and people tend to listen to them.

Many people here are still holding back from forgiving or asking for forgiveness, but the witness of others has softened them. They say things like, "Well, if someone was truly sorry and came to me and asked for forgiveness, I'd forgive them, but until then I can't forgive." Part of them is ready, but they are still caught up in resentment. They want to be sure that the people who wronged them are sorry for what they did, and while we are encouraging those who did wrong to do just that, true biblical forgiveness does not have those requirements.

Small Groups. People need to forgive as much to benefit them as those whom they are forgiving, because the anger they hold inside will eat away at them and destroy them. There are also those who are ready to ask forgiveness, but are still afraid of those who might judge them, or their friends who might be angry with them. To help these people, we formed groups of released prisoners and victims of the genocide to try and engage them in practical reconciliation.

Restitution

Another side of reconciliation is restitution. We are challenging people to make some kind of recompense. It began with building houses for victims. Deo Gashagaza elaborated:

> I remember Bishop John meeting with the prisoners and asking them how they thought they could best demonstrate the change that had happened in them to their home community. And some of the prisoners suggested that they could build houses for those whose homes had been destroyed during the genocide. They wanted to do something for the people they had hurt. They couldn't bring back the ones they had killed, but they could rebuild the houses.

Towards Forgiveness. The Towards Forgiveness housing program turned out to be a great way not only to demonstrate the sincerity of the prisoners about repentance, but also a way for the survivors and the prisoners to develop a new relationship by working side by side on the building projects before the prisoners were released back into the community.

"When the genocide survivors participate in this action," Deo said, "it also demonstrates that they are willing to pardon these men. There is great healing that happens when the prisoners and the survivors come together and they communicate and work together."

Like most of the steps the Prison Fellowship has taken, the Towards Forgiveness program was an instant success.

"There was a big demand right away, and many people wanted to be involved," Deo maintained. "We don't have the funds for the materials to operate this program all across the country, so we chose some pilot provinces. We have five thousand people working in one, and three hundred in another. The program has worked out very well in both of them."

Our desire is to expand this expression of restitution all over the country. If we had the money, we would build such houses in every district, and let the perpetrators who have repented and are coming back into society demonstrate the power of that repentance by doing something practical. They draw water for the people who are working, they bring food for them, and sometimes they eat together.

Ex-prisoner Nemeye Saveri agreed:

The cooperation we experienced during the construction of the houses really helped to close the gap between us and the survivors of the genocide. We used the time we spent together to talk about many things that helped reconcile us. When an old lady would pick up a brick, there would be an ex-convict to help her. The housing project was a blessing because, during the genocide, we not only killed people, but we looted and demolished houses that belonged to Tutsis as well. It was a real blessing to the homeless survivors.

Nemeye is currently at work building a house for Sefa Murego, whose story I told at the beginning of the book. For a long time Sefa was not able to think about Nemeye and the other men who killed her family without feeling a great hatred. She recalled:

Then, one day I was at least able to pray that I would be able to forgive someday. I still couldn't imagine meeting them face-to-face, but when I saw them, God gave me the heart to forgive. At first I just talked with Nemeye and Ndanguza, but when I saw the pain they felt and learned about the changes they'd gone through, I became more open with them.

Then we worked together on the building of my house and I realized that, in a way, they had been victims too. Then I was able to forgive them. I care about the house, yes, but I care more about the changed hearts of the men who are building it for me. I don't know how this happened. It is a miracle, I guess, but we even can laugh together now. And the pain is much less.

Project Dairy Cows. Another program we are developing is to have perpetrators who have repented and victims who have forgiven engage in a productive project together. This is not about restitution or witnessing, but about producing something worthwhile together.

My goal is to establish an association that would help them raise dairy cows together. They would participate in a dairy corporation—learn to raise cows and sell the milk. They would visit each other and encourage each other. They would begin to understand that they are dependent on each other. I have applied to the Heifer Project International to provide cows to begin this program.

This is our mission—to establish three aspects of reconciliation within the community.

- Repentance and forgiveness are a mental exercise and a spiritual exercise of the heart.
- Restitution is taking place as perpetrators build houses for victims.
- A production program needs to be established that will help people relate to one another and remove any lingering suspicions, and also help the nation economically.

The reconciliation ministry is about healing the nation.

The Reconciliation Process

God's Love

The very first step is to help people get over the haunting fear and overwhelming guilt by helping them understand that no matter what they have gone through and no matter what they have done, they are still loved by God. Despite the fact that the pain is unbearable, God loves them. Despite the atrocious thing(s) they did, God has not given up on them. That must be the foundation.

Large Meetings

The best way to initially connect with the people is through a large meeting. They are more likely to attend a meeting if they know a lot of people will be there. It allows them to disappear in a sea of faces. But also it puts perpetrators and survivors together, and we can engage their hearts by presenting topics that help them think about each other. That's the first stage.

Smaller Conferences and Prison Visits

The next phase is to have a smaller conference just for the survivors. We have about forty people come together and stay in the guesthouse on the church compound for two or three days. We are prepared; we understand that they are going to break down as painful memories surface. When we unearth their wounds, they need to cry. We have to let them cry.

At the end of the conference I invite some of them to come to the prisons with me and listen to the preaching. Sitting with the prisoners is very hard for some of them, and not all of them can do it at first. But for those who do come, it can be a very powerful step toward healing. Often some of the prisoners will repent right there and request to ask forgiveness from the survivors.

Every now and then, a prisoner might even know one of the survivors, call him or her by name, and ask forgiveness for hurting his or her family. Sometimes the survivors will respond and say that they are prepared to forgive the person if he or she has truly repented.

During one such situation, a survivor forgave a man who asked for his pardon, and then he saw a boy at the prison whom he said was innocent of doing anything deserving imprisonment. And, not only that, he said he would be willing to help the boy get released. This is the kind of thing that can happen when God begins to heal the pain. That's the power of God! We don't usually put survivors together with those who attacked them at such an early stage, because it can cause a clash, but this was a time when God superseded our normal plan.

Survivors and Perpetrators Meet

Usually we talk to the survivors several times to prepare them to meet with the perpetrators who were involved in the attacks in their area and have asked for forgiveness. We pray with them and talk about Jesus. I usually tell them that I understand their pain, and I share the story of my niece. I cry with them. It's very painful for me, too. I understand their pain. I tell them, "Remember, Jesus did not wait until He was off the cross. He was still in pain when He forgave. The nails were still in His hands. And the crown of thorns was still on His head. They were still mocking Him underneath the cross. And He cried to the Father, saying, 'Father, forgive them.'"

And then I say, "Our pain is still real today, and we need to forgive now! We can't wait until it's over, because it won't go away anyway until we forgive. And we won't be free from the anger until we forgive."

We also talk to the perpetrators several times in preparation for meeting the survivors. We treat each group separately. When both groups are prepared and they ask for the opportunity to meet, then we arrange a meeting. The first time they meet, we don't have them talk about what happened during the genocide. We just have them meet and talk. We try to keep it light.

The second time they meet, we have them talk a little bit about it in general terms. The third time, we help them get into the specifics, the details that cause so much pain. There is a lot of crying. The survivors cry, and the perpetrators cry. That is when forgiveness happens.

Restitution

The next phase is the restitution process. This also involves matching up the perpetrators and the survivors from a given area. When the prisoners from a certain locality are released, we contact the survivors from that locality and arrange for them to meet for the series of meetings I just described. When the perpetrators have asked for forgiveness, the survivors have forgiven them, and they have cried together, then we talk about restitution. We discuss what can be done to help the survivors.

Building a house is a witness of repentance by the perpetrator, and receiving the house is the acceptance of repentance by the survivor. Ultimately that kind of healing cannot be done through human efforts. It is the work of God. And if it is happening in Rwanda, it can happen elsewhere.

Problems Hindering Reconciliation

Reoccupying the Land

A very practical problem for the survivors is reoccupying the land. There is not that much land in Rwanda, and often survivors returned to find their homes claimed by Tutsi refugees from other nations. The refugees tend to settle where their ancestors lived, and many came to Rwanda and found land, but some of that land belonged to people who abandoned it during the genocide. In Rwanda we don't document land ownership. When you consider that 80 percent of Rwanda's population are subsistence farmers, these disputes create real problems. A person cannot just farm anywhere.

Courage to Return

Another problem is having the courage to return. It's extremely difficult to return to the place where your family was killed. Besides the pain, they are no longer with you for support. The government is building townships of thirty to fifty homes on a small piece of land to help provide places for people to live, but that doesn't enable them to farm. Many survivors live in such townships because they can't bear to return to the villages where the massacres occurred. Some of them hire out or sell the land they had in the villages.

Reaching the People

Another large problem is reaching the people. In Rwanda, we don't have much mass media, and the genocide taught people to be suspicious of the media. So you have to go to the people and reach them where they are—in the cities or in the villages, in the flatlands or in the mountains. The same geographical obstacles that required such overwhelming cooperation to make the genocide happen are the same ones we now have to face in bringing about reconciliation. It is easy to get to people in the prisons, but much harder to reach the others who are scattered.

Holding On to Hatred

The greatest barrier to reconciliation, however, is that so many people refuse to give up their hatred. We have tried to convince people that the work of reconciliation is as urgent as anything being done Rwanda. The more we delay, the more we will have to overcome, but it is difficult. There are some Hutu extremists who are not yet repentant.

Some of them claim to believe that what they were doing was right, but this only shows the depth of their denial. It has gone deep into their consciences and their minds. The more they deny, the more they sink into guilt. Because of the laws here, they can't proclaim their hatred like before, but it is still there. Many have accepted denial as the normal way of living, and the more they cover the pain, the more dangerous it is for Rwanda.

If they are not dealt with, these repressed feelings will burst forth and cause more violence. There are also victims of the genocide who are still very angry. Sometimes people are hesitant to forgive because they think they are belittling the loss of their loved ones by forgiving those who harmed them. But that is another lie from the pit. These are separate issues.

For a woman to forgive the person who killed her son does not take away from who her son was. It does not make her son less important. Forgiving something does not make the forgiven act less horrible, but it does break the power that act holds over you. The truth is that those who don't forgive are dying from their unforgiveness. The bitterness eats them up. When you forgive, you are healthier and more alive.

Pastor Steven Gahigi is part of the prison ministry and a living testament to God's healing power.

My family was killed in the genocide. When the RPF came into power, I returned to Rwanda, but all I thought about was revenge. So many lives were lost, so much misery was created, I just wanted to punish those who had killed. I had been a preacher, and I spent many hours asking God how He could have allowed such a thing. Then God showed me that people who killed in the genocide did so because they didn't know God. And now God was asking me to help them know Him. That's how I was able to go to the prison to preach.

It was not easy, because I had to put aside my feelings and trust God. But then I was able to see God's transforming power. Then came the day when I saw one of the people who killed my family and God told me to forgive him. I didn't think I could do it, but when the man saw me and asked for my forgiveness, God gave me the grace to do it. And then I began to heal inside.

Pastor Gahigi often compares Rwanda to the biblical story of Jacob and Esau:

They were brothers, but one was forced to go into exile because he feared death at the hands of his brother. But when Jacob returned from exile, he reconciled with his brother and they hugged one another. As long as there is genuine repentance, openly and verbally, where all parties accept their wrongdoing, then we will have hope for our nation. Getting survivors together with those who killed innocent people was the result of God's grace.

Steven Gahigi also sees the bright future that God has in store for this nation:

Through the Prison Fellowship and some of the other programs Bishop John is doing, we are moving towards peace in Rwanda, but we want to go even beyond peace and have all Rwandese together in good relationship. We want to show the children that their future will not be like the past. Their children will not suffer the way they have and that the future of Rwanda is very promising because Rwanda is turning to God and God is good.

Fear

Fear is also a huge barrier. First of all, there is the fear of change. People naturally fear change, especially when that change requires them to take a step such as forgiving or asking for forgiveness. In every community, people know many people who were with them when they did evil, and they are afraid that those people may attack them, or criticize and harass them if they repent. Others worry that they will turn them in, now that they have repented.

I tell them that after we leave there will be people who will tell them not to repent, but these people are deceiving them: "They are afraid and their fear is perpetuating your pain, making it last longer. They're killing you." Sometimes people who are afraid repent inside. They crave the courage to shake off their guilt and be free because they have seen people who have done it, but they still fear their contemporaries. This is where the majority of Rwanda is today.

Yesterday's Path of Division / Today's Path of Healing

These are some of the battles we are facing. But we are committed through the Lord Jesus Christ, to continue to foster the reconciliation. We will continue to hold conferences and try to reach people. We will try to show them how the resentment between Hutu and Tutsi was manufactured and created by the colonists. Then it became a reality. They turned it into a creed and then they executed it.

Rwanda spent millions of dollars and millions of hours of manpower spreading a message of division and then taking it to the worst place possible. Now we must spend dollars and manpower healing the nation. The former government spent money to teach and train the militia and the death squads. Now we need to spend money to teach and train volunteers to bring about reconciliation.

The country never advanced the way it should, because so much energy went into hate. No one was really striving to make the society better. Many people in Rwanda still have no shoes, and we have been independent since 1962. More than forty-four years and we have not been able to even provide shoes for our people! But all of that is about to change. Rwanda is on the path of healing and on the path of blessing. God is blessing Rwanda again.

ELEVEN

Forgiveness

The Apologies

By the end of 1997, the international community realized that the new Rwanda was a reality, and prominent political figures began to apologize for their lack of action during the genocide. One of the first was former Secretary of State of the United States Madeleine Albright, who authored so many denials and engineered so many delays to keep America from coming to our aid during the genocide.

She delivered a speech to the Organization of African Unity in Addis Ababa in which she said: "We—the international community—should have been more active in the early stages of the atrocities in Rwanda in 1994 and called them what they were: genocide." [1] She then made a brief visit to Rwanda, during which she also condemned the use of humanitarian aid "to sustain armed camps or to support genocidal killers." [2]

Albright's "apology," as we Rwandans took it to be, was a breakthrough of sorts in that it was one of the first times a significant member of the international community moved away from a defensive denial of the Rwandan genocide and began to accept it as fact.

President Bill Clinton came three months later and became the first Western head of state to visit Rwanda after the genocide. On March 25, 1998, he landed at the airport and spent several hours listening to stories of some survivors of the genocide, and then made an impassioned speech during which he apologized for refusing to intervene during the slaughter and for supporting the killers in the camps.

"During the ninety days that began on April 6 in 1994, Rwanda experienced the most intensive slaughter in this blood-filled century," Clinton said. "It is important that the world know that these killings were not spontaneous or accidental . . . they were most certainly not the result of ancient tribal struggles . . . These events grew from a policy aimed at the systematic destruction of a people."[3]

And this mattered not only to Rwanda but also to the world, he explained, because "each bloodletting hastens the next as the value of human life is degraded and violence becomes tolerated, the unimaginable becomes more conceivable."[4]

Clinton did not duck the international community's responsibility, saying:

The international community, together with nations in Africa, must bear its share of responsibility for this tragedy, as well. We did not act quickly enough after the killing began. We should not have allowed the refugee camps to become safe havens for the killers. We did not immediately call these crimes by their rightful name: genocide. We cannot change the past. But we can and must do everything in our power to help you build a future without fear, and full of hope.[5]

I've met Bill Clinton three times, and even though he refused to send help during the genocide, he did have the courage to come to Rwanda and apologize publicly for his negligence. And he even appeared on CNN and admitted he made a mistake, saying that he considered failing to help Rwanda during the genocide the worst mistake of his presidency. He has come to Rwanda twice since then and was very active both in pressing the UN to conduct an official inquiry into the genocide and in establishing the HIV treatment program here. Consequently, I believe his apology was sincere.

Even so, those of us in Rwanda hope that the rest of the world realizes that you cannot depend upon the international community for protection. On the morning of Albright's visit, Hutu Power advocates, shouting, "Kill the cock-roaches!" hacked and shot to death more than three hundred Tutsis at a northwestern encampment named Mudende. A few days before Clinton came, fifty Tutsis were killed in similar massacres at Janda. Rwanda must be diligent enough and strong enough to protect itself. That is the only way that peace can be guaranteed.

On May 7, 1998, United Nations secretary-general Kofi Annan came to Kigali and apologized to the parliament of Rwanda:

> The world must deeply repent this failure. Rwanda's tragedy was the world's tragedy. All of us who cared about Rwanda, all of us who witnessed its suf-fering, fervently wish that we could have prevented the genocide. Looking back now, we see the signs which then were not recognized. Now we know that what we did was not nearly enough—not enough to save Rwanda from itself, not enough to honour the ideals for which the United Nations exists. We will not deny that, in their greatest hour of need, the world failed the people of Rwanda.[6]

It is hard for someone in power to admit that his or her negligence or polit-ical concerns could have played even a small part in the deaths of so many, but it is harder still to have endured the experience, knowing that your pleas for help fell on deaf ears. General Dallaire suffered a mental breakdown after he left Rwanda and twice attempted suicide to escape the anguish of his memo-ries. Now recovered, he wrote the following in *Shake Hands with the Devil*:

> As I write these words I am listening to Samuel Barber's *Adagio for Strings*, which strikes me as the purest expression in music of the suffering, mutilation, rape, and murder of 800,000 Rwandans, with the help of the member nations of the only supposedly impartial world body. Ultimately, led by the United States, France and the United Kingdom, this world body aided and abetted

genocide in Rwanda. No amount of its cash and aid will ever wash its hands clean of Rwandan blood.[7]

Only God Changes Hearts

The hope for Rwanda does not lie in the hands of the international community. The hope for Rwanda lies in the hands of a God who is capable of changing human hearts. In April 1997, a group of *genocidaires* killed sixteen students and injured twenty at a boarding school in Kibuye and a few weeks later murdered seventeen girls and a sixty-two-year-old Belgian nun at a similar school in Gisenyi.

In both instances the group of 150 Interahamwe and former RGF troops roused the students from their sleep and ordered them to separate into Hutus and Tutsis. The students refused to separate, saying that they were simply Rwandans, so they were beaten and shot indiscriminately. There is nothing that evil can do in the face of such courage.

Two days after the second attack, some of the killers came forth and confessed. Unable to divide the school children, the Hutu Power advocates murdered many Hutus and were overcome by remorse. That is the power of God. And that is the only power that can save Rwanda.

My wife, Harriet, spent almost three years in near trauma after she saw a video of babies being killed. She just couldn't forgive women who had babies themselves killing other babies. When we were at Pawleys Island, South Carolina, God spoke to her. She was down by the water and saw a dog playing with a group of birds. The dog was running at the birds and barking, and the birds flew away just far enough so that the dog could come at them again. Sometimes the birds would fly right at the dog so that he would chase them again.

And the Lord spoke to her and said, *If birds can play with that dog, how is it that the people in your country fail to work together?* She realized that if dogs and birds, natural enemies, can play together, then she must forgive and forget. And she was healed through that, but it was not easy going. We have a long way to go in Rwanda, but reconciliation is happening, and if it can happen here, it can happen anywhere.

Evangelistic Ministry

I believe that the best way to promote peace and forgiveness in Rwanda is to convert people to Jesus. For years the churches here boasted of Rwandans knowing Jesus, but if the people of Rwanda had truly accepted Christ into their hearts, there would have been no genocide. People who truly know Jesus Christ as their Lord and Savior, undergo a transformation from within. The Holy Scriptures—not their hate and prejudices—guide them.

Leading people to Christ goes beyond the walls of the church to the people of our nation, wherever we find them. The pastors, priests, and ministers throughout Rwanda must stop propagating religion or "churchianity" and promote true Christianity.

I am the chairman of a group of sixteen protestant churches, different denominations that have come together to work on evangelism in Rwanda. Our choirs perform together. One method of evangelism is to tell people that their religious animosity should come to an end. Some of the missionaries who came from the colonial powers to Africa didn't really teach us Jesus. They taught us their hostilities.

People from different religions were killing each other in Europe, and some of that hatred transferred into the conversions in Rwanda and elsewhere in Africa. They were herding people into religion, but not converting them to Jesus. The churches were more concerned with politics and power than with love and healing. They lost the ability to love and disciple the people. It's the same in America today, where the churches have all the finances and material they need to evangelize and disciple the entire country, but they have embraced power and politics instead.

We have preached the gospel in crusades that have grown from the local church level to the parish level and on to the archdeacon level. July 2005, we held a crusade throughout the entire diocese. We had anticipated and planned for four thousand people, but ten thousand attended. The theme of that crusade was simply, "We Want to See Jesus."

Our goal is not to have big, religious churches, but to have a Christian community of believers who put their faith into practice. Christianity is not just a philosophy. It is life. I smile it. I speak it. I live it. I relate it to other

people. It is not about being religious as it was in the early days when missionaries came to Rwanda and made so many converts that turned out to be in
name only.

It is about new life and freedom—the freedom to love others the way God
loves us, the freedom to forgive and to be forgiven. That is what Christianity
must be in Rwanda. Only Jesus can turn hearts and minds from hate to love,
from sorrow and pain to freedom and joy. Because we know that, we are no
longer about pleasing the world or pleasing people with money or power. We are
about pleasing Christ, because that is who our healing comes from.

The Gacacha Courts

The Gacacha courts began in 2003 as a way for the community to work
together to investigate and reveal the truth about the genocide. *Gacacha* is the
name of the grass that grows in the community compounds. Historically,
Rwandans sat on gacacha to testify and work out their problems. When there
was a grudge between people, they came together and sat on the grass around
the compound to discuss it.

The Arusha courts that were formed by the international community to
prosecute the perpetrators of the genocide were in Tanzania, far away from
the people of the villages. The people of Rwanda had little control over what
happened in Arusha, and there were many problems and injustices. The
Rwandan government decided to hold their own courts the old-fashioned
way, by having a tribunal of people from each area hear the testimony of the
local people, and questioning those under suspicion. The process began in a
few villages on an experimental basis, but proved so successful that it was
soon expanded to one village in each province, and now it is in every district
in the country.

The entire community participates in the gacacha courts. Anyone who
attends—from the village elder to the youngest child—may ask questions.
There is a group of six or so people who have been elected by the people and
trained by the government to preside over the court and lead the investigation.

They begin by collecting information on the genocide in that parish or village from every source available. Then they hold the hearings in the open, where everyone can attend, and they question people.

The process restores the responsibility of protecting the community to the people of that community. The people who are asking the questions are from the community, and the people who are giving the information are from the community. The sense of community is preserved, and that is very important in Rwanda, because even if someone goes to jail, he will return to the same community when he is released.

Those who have done wrong are brought to justice by the community. If you offended the community, the community judges you, and eventually it is that same community that restores you and welcomes you back. By allowing the people in the community to question someone who is suspected of perpetrating the genocide, the anger and resentment are greatly relieved because they have been expressed. In asking these questions the people are airing their sorrow, and that helps to relieve it.

The Gacacha courts also provide more opportunity for people to repent. Since people from the same villages are there, they are helping each other to be accountable. A person may try to conceal some things, but then someone in the crowd will say, "Wait! You were at a roadblock, and you had a gun! I saw it. What did you use that gun for?" Or a person might say, "I just looted." But someone else says, "No, my friend, we were together. We killed so-and-so together. I hit him on the head, and you speared him."

This process helps people to unearth the truth, to overcome denial, and to move toward repentance. The community remembers what happened. People do not forget something that their hearts remind them of every single day. The pain and the guilt make them remember vividly.

The Future of Genocide

Contrary to what most people believe, genocides are on the increase, and experts predict that they will continue to increase. The genocide in Rwanda proves that this increase is not because of better weapons. There were no weapons of mass destruction used in Rwanda. The chief weapon of genocide is hatred. Genocide is often a product of political corruption combined with some form of prejudice.

In modern society, genocide is most prevalent in underdeveloped areas or nations. Failed development leaves states vulnerable to genocide because they become dependent on other countries. This sometimes brings about a mind-set of racial superiority, which can lead to hatred and violence when certain criteria come into play.

Eight Stages of Genocide

According to Gregory Stanton, the president of the Genocide Watch, genocide develops in eight stages that he said are "predictable but not inexorable."[8] That means we can stop this horrible crime against humanity if we recognize it in time. Following are the stages of genocide and the preventive measures that can be taken at each stage.

1. *Classification.* The first stage involves dividing people into groups, usually with the "us and them" type of mentality. The primary preventive measure at this early stage is to develop universal institutions that transcend division. (In Rwanda this would have meant abolishing identity cards that marked a person as a Hutu or Tutsi.)

2. *Symbolization.* This involves developing symbols that serve as signs of resentment for the targeted group. To combat this phase such symbols can be legally forbidden. (In Rwanda, the former national flag and national anthem were hate symbols.)

3. *Dehumanization.* This is where propaganda is first used to overcome the normal human revulsion against murder. To prevent this stage, hate propaganda must be banned and hate crimes promptly punished. (In Rwanda, dehumanizing political cartoons were published and soon grew in popularity.)

4. *Organization.* Genocide requires a great deal of organization. During this phase special army units or militia are trained and armed. The only way to combat this stage is to outlaw membership in such groups. (In Rwanda, the Interahamwe were developed during this phase.)

5. *Polarization.* This happens when propaganda moves into the broadcast and national publication level. Not only should hate broadcasts and publications be outlawed to combat this stage, but by this time there probably is also a need for security protection for moderate leaders and human rights groups. (Radio RTMLC played a major part in the genocide in Rwanda, as did many propaganda-filled publications.)

6. *Identification.* At this stage the targeted victims are identified and separated from others because of their ethnic or religious identity. A genocide alert must be called. It is important that as many people as possible, especially those in the targeted group, be aware that the killings are imminent. (In Rwanda, the identity cards also figured in this stage, but in many cases this was extended to a house-by-house registration of Tutsis so that their exact locations could be handed over to the killers.)

7. *Extermination.* The perpetrators of genocide consider mass murder as extermination, and the only thing that can stop it at this point is rapid and overwhelming armed intervention that includes the establishment of safe areas and refugee escape corridors with armed protection. (The killings in Rwanda were done on a mass scale with no planned safe area or routes of escape.)

8. *Denial.* During the final stage of genocide, the perpetrators deny that they have committed any crime. Such criminals must be tried and punished by an international tribunal, national courts, or both. (This is still being done in Rwanda.)

Genocide in Darfur

As of this writing, the genocide in Darfur continues with no signs of abating. This is another case of genocide caused in part by failed development.

The problem in this area of western Sudan began as a conflict between two ethnic groups as they competed for land and water. Violence and destruction have raged in Darfur since February 2003. Government-sponsored militias known as the Janjaweed have conducted a calculated campaign of slaughter, rape, starvation, and displacement in Darfur.

More than four hundred thousand people have died because of the violence and the resulting starvation and disease. More than 2.5 million people have been displaced from their homes. More than two hundred thousand live in refugee camps across the border in Chad—lacking adequate food, shelter, sanitation, and health care. Although the United States Congress and President George W. Bush have recognized the situation in Darfur as genocide and declared it the worst humanitarian crisis in the world at this time, little is being done to stop it.

The only solution to genocide is an international desire to end it and take the necessary steps to do so. The UN has created laws addressing international peace, but the laws are ineffective if they are not acted upon.

TWELVE

The Future

Rwanda Is Blessed

Spiritual Blessings

It is hard for people to understand when I speak of Rwanda as a nation that is being blessed by God, but it is true. Since the genocide, God has touched our nation in so many ways. I have witnessed so many miracles of healing and forgiveness that I could not possibly recount them all. There is no pain greater than seeing your loved ones tortured and killed before your eyes, yet God has healed countless numbers of Rwandans of such pain. He has put their hearts and minds at ease, giving them the peace that "surpasses all understanding" discussed in the Bible (Philippians 4:7 NKJV).

What could be worse than the horrible emotional anguish of undeniable guilt that replays over and over the terrible acts of violence committed against innocents—even small children and babies? Yet God has healed the hearts and minds of many who performed such atrocities, because they confessed their guilt and called upon Him in faith to forgive them.

Economic Blessings

Not all of Rwanda's blessings require spiritual eyes to see. Rwanda always had great potential. Here was an African country where everyone spoke the same language (very unusual), where the land was very fertile, and where the people had a long-standing culture of obedience. In my seminars I usually tell people that the devil hates good things, so he worked extra hard to turn those positive things into a negative. He found a way to divide us so that our strengths turned against us. But God has redeemed Rwanda in not only spiritual ways, but in economic ones as well.

Today, Rwanda is rated as having the best communication system in Africa. If you go the Intercontinental Hotel, you don't have to plug your laptop into the wall in order to retrieve your e-mail. You can go anywhere in the hotel. It's all wireless! And we are doing this everywhere. It's the same with telephones. Instead of setting up landlines in places where we have never had service, we are moving right to cellular technology. There are many people here using cell phones who never had a landline phone in their life.

Governance Blessings

We were recently graded first in good governance as well. The Rwandan government has decentralized the leadership, and local people are taking part in their own governance. They are helping to determine the priorities in the country's development and in the management of our resources. The economy is growing much faster than anybody could have expected. Just a decade after the genocide, our country was raising a good percentage of our budget from our own taxes. That had never been done before in the history of Rwanda.

We are building roads. The head of the UNICEF mission is working with us at a district level to help decide what project would be the best for them to do. Those decisions used to be declared by the cabinet ministers in Kigali, but now they are being done at a district level, which shows that the decentralization of the government has been effective. Our new constitution has provisions for the local people to decide the course of their development along with trained and professional planners.

The Rwandan Army is one of the most organized and disciplined in the world. It is composed of both Hutus and Tutsis working together. The army has embraced all the values and programs of reconciliation and has incorporated them into their policies.

People are working together in Rwanda more than ever. It is the result of good leadership. The people of Rwanda are starting to realize how much they lost by not having such leadership in the past. The first thirty-four years of our independence were spent bickering, betraying, exploiting, depriving, and killing people. If we had had good leadership during that time, this country would be one of the major developed countries in Africa.

Most people realize that we have an opportunity in Rwanda, which we never had before, and are trying their best to make the most of it. We have free elections. In the last election, a candidate came in from Brussels who advocated division and violence, and the people did not accept him. He thought because he was a Hutu that the people would accept his ideas about ethnic divisions, but the people have grown. Even those in the outlying districts will not accept this kind of thinking again.

President Kagame was a refugee all of his life. His youth was spent in a refugee camp where he was barefoot. He was hungry like all the other refugees in the camp. He went into the bush for a number of years in Uganda and in Rwanda. He fought for liberation and the freedom of humankind on different fronts. Now he has risen to the presidency, and he listens to God through all that experience.

He knows what brokenness and poverty are, and he sees no reason for that to be the destiny of Rwanda's people. Why should our children suffer the same fate we suffered when we can build a nation that provides for them?

Making Progress

Of course, there are still echoes from the past. Those who helped design and organize the genocide and fled to Europe and other places have no concept of what's going on here. They still speak evil of Rwanda. They hoarded enough money from exploiting the people to escape into wealthy lifestyles in other countries. They are still bickering and sending e-mails complaining against the new government. Their effect is less because the world is watching. World leaders now visit Rwanda regularly and are astounded at our progress.

Rwandans are still returning home. Recently a group of eight people came from the Congo representing seven thousand Rwandan refugees. They asked the government to give them permission to come and see for themselves if the country is peaceful, if the development they are hearing about on the radio is true, so that they can go and tell their brothers to come home. They spent a week traveling all over the country, and then they went back to the camp at Prezorville. At the airport they said, "We cannot believe what we have seen. We cannot believe this amount of peace. The country's changed. We must tell everyone to come home!"

There are countries in Africa that are rich in natural resources, but extremely poor in managing those resources because of poor policies and poor leadership. There are also countries that are poor in natural resources, but better in managing because they have learned to manage very well the little they have.

Our president says that Rwanda is not as poor as the world thinks. He says that the greatest resource Rwanda has is its people, and it is the goal of the government to help our brains work productively to produce wealth. Instead of engaging our brains, strength, and energy in something negative, we must use these things positively. Instead of destroying the little we have, we must work to build.

So we in Rwanda today believe we are richer than the Congolese, who have oil, timber, many minerals, and lots of good land. Because they have had poor management, the wealth that was available to them has been lost and looted. Soon the Congo will sell us timber, and we will sell them our expertise to help them have electricity and better communications in their country. The Congo, Tanzania, Kenya, and other countries will get it from us, because we will have the best. We will produce the cell phones here and all the related forms of that technology. In today's world, wealth is not just about having resources, but also about having the expertise to put them to good use.

Forgiveness of Debts

Rwanda has also been blessed in that their international debt to the World Bank, IMF, and other monetary institutions has been forgiven. Some of these debts were actually from the cost of the genocide. Some were related to the cost of guns and other weapons, the cost of hiring France to train the militia to kill their own people, and other debts that were accumulated during the genocide. When you inherit a government, you inherit the debts. So Kagame had to pay the debts that were acquired to kill a million people.

Aid from Friends

Besides this, Rwanda is receiving aid from several friendly countries. The United Kingdom's Department for International Development (DFID) announced July 2005 that they have set aside more than four million pounds to improve the social welfare of genocide survivors who were infected and affected by HIV/AIDS. Many others are contributing as well.

Divine Blessings

The economists may not understand this aspect of our development, but I believe God is blessing Rwanda not just to make up for the horrible things that happened, but because we have earnestly sought Him as a nation, and we have tried to apply His principles to the way we do things as a country. God uses the broken to bring Him glory. God sometimes uses the uneducated or the hopeless and blesses them so that the world may know God is the Almighty.

God uses the weak to shame the strong. Gideon, for example, was hopelessly outnumbered, and yet God told him to reduce the size of his army. He said, "Tell those who are fearing, trembling from inside, to go home" and then He said, "There are still too many. Take them to the well. Separate those who are drinking from their hands from those who are licking like dogs." In the end only three hundred people remained with Gideon. Then God said He would do a miracle with the three hundred. He used the least—the smallest number—to defeat the enemy. God picked a group of Galilean fishermen to turn the world upside down with the gospel of Jesus.

Rwandans must develop a clear direction of where they want the country to go and be able to stand firm in that vision in order to make the country what God wants it to be. If we do, it's possible that God will use poor little Rwanda to do miracles all over the world. Then the world will know that it's not the power of men, but His divine provision that has made such a thing happen.

I spoke at a college commencement program in America and told the students how the economy of Uganda was devastated during the reign of Idi Amin. I told them that sometimes the stagnation or the destruction of the economy may depend on beliefs of the people who make up that economy. Their beliefs, vision, attitude, and commitment affect not only their economy, but also their history.

Americans are enjoying the fruit of the beliefs and the attitudes of their forefathers. Because the founders of America wanted the country to be like the biblical model of a town built on the top of the hill to be seen by everyone as a place of freedom and justice, God blessed America. The people worked for it, and God blessed that work. They had faith in Him, and He helped them build the United States into the great nation it is today. I warned them that if America now says it believes in nothing, then the economy and their future history may lead to nothing.

Building Programs

We are now in the eighth year of our programs. I have an extensive plan for development in many areas, but that plan has to be executed very slowly at times. Part of our mission statement is to educate the people to save them from being so easily manipulated and exploited, not just spiritually, but also socially, economically, and politically. That means rehabilitating old schools and constructing new ones. Therefore, we have invested in many schools.

Schools

First, we built the Sonrise Elementary School in 2002, which is a boarding school for students from the first through sixth grades. When the children reached the sixth grade, we realized that if we released them at such an early age, they would not have enough education to establish a culture strong enough to survive the pressures in the community. By providing school beyond sixth grade, we can help children form a mature character that may not be so easily overcome by the pressures of living in the community. So we are currently in the process of building Sonrise High School, beginning with the seventh grade. I'm happy to say that those who have completed the first six years of our school took the national exam last year and finished third in the nation. Right now we have five hundred students from the first grade to the seventh.

The Minister of Education has already approved a few additional years beyond that. Our new policy takes them through ninth grade, and we plan on having tenth, eleventh, and twelfth grades available to them as well. Then when they finish the twelfth grade, we can release them into the universities. We are hoping to build Sonrise Technical Institute for those who are not able to go to the universities. That way we can teach them a professional trade, such as mechanical engineering or carpentry. By the time they finish their education, we want them to be able to earn a living.

Sonrise Elementary is a school primarily composed of orphans whose parents died in the genocide, but there are children whose parents were perpetrators as well. Some of these parents left the country, and some of them died in the jungles, but the children are innocent Rwandans who need help and love. It doesn't matter whether the father died doing evil or if the father was innocently killed. His child is an orphan.

We also have some children whose parents were killed in the late nineties by Interahamwe who came over from the Congo to attack. We are raising them all as the children of Rwanda, citizens of this nation. This is practical reconciliation. When they grow up, they will not see things as Amatutsi or Amahutu. They will have grown together. They have been loved the same way, fed the same way, clothed the same way, and educated the same way. We teach them the sad history of Rwanda, and we tell them they are to be pillars of the new nation. When these children graduate into universities and go out into the community, we will have a class of people who understand what it is to be a good citizen of this country.

While the Sonrise schools are set up to accommodate orphans, they are not orphanages—for a very good reason. We are trying to foster family relationships. We want these children to connect with what family members they might have, so that those relationships can be built. I realized that connecting with family is one of the practical means for healing the people. Not only does it engage reconciliation, but it is also a way of witnessing to the general community to show them that things can be restored back to normal.

By having children from all walks of life, we establish reconciliation and then spread it back into the community at large. These children come home with changed behavior, with good thinking, with a witness for life, and they share their bright hope with others. Releasing five hundred students into the homes of this region for a month, makes a huge difference in the community. Then we bring the children back to the school again for another three months, where we love and care for them, and then release them into the community again for another month. This is an ongoing witness, and it has had a tremendous influence.

If I had the funds, I would build at least three more schools so there would be at least one in each of the provinces that our diocese covers. We are also very involved in the refurbishing of schools all over the diocese. We have launched a fund-raising campaign to fix up the old schools. We have already begun refurbishing sixty-six elementary schools. We also built a few new public schools. The Anglican Church built them, but the Rwandan government will pay for the teachers and the syllabi.

Churches

In the early years of my ministry here, we worked so hard on the schools that a lot of people thought I had forgotten that we needed a church. I was using the old church all the time, and it was too small and not really adequate for our needs. People said that this bishop didn't see the need for a new church. I replied, "No, I see it, but God does not want me to make the building a priority. I'm building the church by building schools. I'm building the church by repairing the hospital. I'm building the church by taking care of remote areas where children have nothing and we are losing generations of youths. Therefore I am building the church first. Then, after I build the church, I will build the building."

Looking Back

Sonrise School

It is so much easier to look back now on all that we have done and thank God for it, than it was to look ahead and praise Him when all we had were dreams and plans. I remember one time after I had thought about building the Sonrise School, I paid the little money I had to an architect to draw up some plans and pictures for me. I showed the plans to the executive secretary general of the Unity and Reconciliation program. I told her the plan I had for the reconciliation of the nation, which was a long-term project. The plan was to get as many of the orphans together as we could, heal them of the trauma, teach them about the history of the country, give them the best education we could, help them to build a wonderful character, and develop them as the best citizens we could possibly make them.

Then we could build a united community through these children. She looked at my plans and gave me her full attention. Then she said, "John, you really have wonderful thoughts. The plan is excellent, but you are too ambitious. You will never achieve this. This is too big for a human mind to achieve. You can't afford it."

But I said, "Ma'am, if it's from me, I may not achieve it. But if it's from God and if it is for the benefit of the people of Rwanda, it will be done."

I had hoped that I could get at least half of the money from this lady's office to build that school, but she told me it was too ambitious. She didn't offer to cooperate. She didn't even say, "We shall pray for you" or encourage me at all. She just said, "This is not achievable."

Two years later, when the building was completed, I invited her to see it. I was recruiting teachers and wanted to start recruiting the orphans. I invited her to come, and I took her around the school. She saw everything. Then she said, "Forgive me for my unbelief."

But the day when I had spoken with her in her office, I drove back home through risks and dangers, with a lot of doubts. When I got home, I went to my knees. I prayed and cried out to the Lord: "Lord, this vision is yours. These orphans are yours. We need to have at least something exemplary in this country."

After some time of prayer, I felt comforted and that I should keep going, keep sharing the vision with people. Then, not too long after that, after a meeting I had in America, I was sitting on the veranda with my wife, and we were talking with a man and a woman who had come to see me. I told them of my dream for the orphans and of my agony and disappointments. I told them about my doubts and confusion and the pain I had for this vision, this project that was not going to be implemented because I didn't have the money.

As we were talking, one of them said, "That school will be called Sonrise. The Son of God must rise into this problem." Then these people said they wanted to be part of making the dream happen. Within two years from that moment on the veranda, the school was completed. After such discouragement, I became so encouraged. From that moment on the veranda we built a sponsorship program and shared it with the people and churches, and it came to pass. The vision was accomplished!

When I get a vision for something, I test it. Who are the beneficiaries? Is this vision meant for me or for the people? Do the people need it? Who's going to be lifted up? Is it the name of God and the people? Is it for my own aggrandizement? Who does this vision serve? If I realize that the vision will benefit the people and the glory will go to the Lord, I know God will bless it.

Computer Library

I talked with a friend about my vision to have the students who graduate from our high school go on to the universities with a good amount of computer skills. We talked about a library where we could put these computers. And that very evening he said, "How much do you think this would cost?" He gave us one hundred thousand dollars to build the library and purchase the computers.

I didn't have the money. But I had the vision. I don't have to have the money. But I do have to pray to the Lord to teach me to communicate the vision. God knows who has the money to see the vision through and bless the people God wants to bless with it. But God gives me my part to play, and my part is to have the vision and manage the vision after it is realized.

Guesthouse

Our guesthouse is a good example of the process involved in seeing a vision realized. First, we recognized the need. Many people travel from Kigali to Ruhengeri. Some are tourists visiting the Diane Fosse National Gorilla Park, which is right next to the church compound. Others are people traveling on to Uganda. And many people from outside the country come to visit us and our church.

Before the guesthouse was built there was nowhere for these people to stay. So I prayed for an opportunity to build something where people coming into the region could sleep and have a hot meal. We have gardens all over the compound, and my wife used to have a large sweet potato garden where I put the guesthouse, so I had to convince her that God was not calling her for the production of sweet potatoes, but had a higher purpose for that spot of land.

Eventually, God showed me how to raise the funds we needed, and we were able to build the guesthouse on the church's compound. The vision became a reality. The guesthouse provides a haven for many people. We want people to see the beautiful mountains of Rwanda and experience how wonderful the people are.

Besides having rooms available in the guesthouse, we allow campers to put up their tents on the lawn, inside the safety of the compound, and provide a place for people to park their recreational vehicles, take showers, and obtain water and hot food. We opened the guesthouse around the same time we opened the Sonrise School. President Kagame came to officially open the school and was the first person to stay in the guesthouse.

Health Services and a New Cathedral

We also rehabilitated Shyira Hospital, Nyange Health Center, and Bigogwe Health Center, which provide health services through the church to the community. By then our old church was in pretty bad shape. So we prayed and felt God was giving us the freedom and the joy to start building the cathedral. It opened on the July 25, 2004. Four thousand people attended a crusade we held that began on July 21 and continued until July 25, the official opening of the cathedral. One day after the cathedral was built, the people reminded me that when we first came here, I had a vision of what God wanted us to do. They said, "This is what you told us. This is what you saw in a vision." But it wasn't like the dream Joseph had in the Bible. It was just God showing me all the possibilities of what we could do. And it came to pass.

Family Blessings

My family is also a great blessing, our nine children, including my late brother's children, whom we adopted. We have been blessed with grand-children as well. We thank God for being able to serve Him with a family who loves Jesus. The Lord has been gracious.

Growth of the People

We have built many churches throughout our diocese, but what is much more important is how we have helped build the people. Although asking Jesus Christ into your heart and accepting that He died for your sins is the most important single thing a person can do, because it gives you eternal life and leads you to victory in this life, our church also tries to address the practical needs of our people. For example, I now have it a policy at our church that we never confirm anyone who can't read. A Christian who doesn't read has a much harder time growing deeper in his or her relationship with the Lord.

Literacy. How can people grow in the service of God if they can't read the Scriptures? How can they sing praises to God if they can't read the hymn-books? How can they be witnesses and teach their family members if they can't share the Word of God with them? Almost 60 percent of our population can't read and write, so our church has a literacy campaign as part of our mission statement.

Economic Growth. We challenge our people to develop. They must have a strategic plan for their personal development. They cannot be satisfied with living in poverty anymore. They have to be motivated to work and claim the statement of Jesus that He came so that they may have life and have it abundantly (John 10:10). You can't have an abundant life when you are living in poverty—or when you are lazy or don't produce. It is the will of God that our people grow economically.

Those of us in leadership in the churches must move beyond the superficial and not be afraid to address the real needs of the people. God will provide in those areas, too. I have seen it. If God gives us a vision, we must have the courage to follow it. If we do, God will see it through to completion.

EPILOGUE

Reconciliation for All

THE STEPS THAT WE ARE USING IN RWANDA FOR RECONCILIATION AND healing can be applied to other communities in the world. There is no barrier that cannot be overcome and no division that cannot be healed. What could be worse than the violence that happened in Rwanda? If the Rwandan situation can be amended by repentance and forgiveness, and the people here can be reconciled enough to live together again, it can happen anywhere in the world. Perhaps differences in culture may require different applications of these methods, but the principle is the same.

The principle is that God can and will heal a human mind no matter how much pain it has seen or caused. God can transform that mind. If a perpetrator of the genocide in Rwanda, a person who tortured and killed many innocent people, including women and children, can repent and cry out for forgiveness to those he wronged by killing their family members, then any offender, anywhere, can repent the same way.

If a woman who was raped and beaten and forced to watch as her husband and children were tortured and killed before her very eyes can forgive in the name of Jesus Christ those who did such a horrible thing, then any victim, anywhere, can forgive the same way.

It is through this repentance and forgiveness that people can relate again. They can live life together again. No one believed that this could happen in

Rwanda. Everyone said, "It's impossible. These people cannot be together again."

It is hard, but it is not impossible—we are doing it!

We have a group of people coming from Ireland to learn about our reconciliation programs. They want to understand how we have achieved so much in such a short time. They are better educated and much wealthier than the people in our country, but they are still fighting in the name of religion. They want to know how we accomplished in eleven short years something that they have been struggling with for hundreds of years. We are anxious to talk with them, to sit and pray with them. We are going to tell them our hope.

With God, all things are possible. We are moving beyond the first encounters between victim and perpetrator to a place where these people can attend church and worship together—they can sing in the same choirs, shop in the same markets, play together on the same sports teams, work next to each other on the job, and eat with each other at home in their villages. If they can afford to forgive, why can't the world forgive?

There are people in our army today who used to fight against that same army. They were captured on the battlefield and rehabilitated to the point where they want to join the very same army they once fought against. And they are the best-disciplined army in the world.

There cannot be any cruelty greater than the cruelty that was in Rwanda, and therefore there is no grace greater than the grace that is in Rwanda. It is a grace that frees people from great cruelty and allows them to share life. And that grace comes from the cross of Jesus Christ. There is no magic here. It's the power of the divine grace of the Lord Jesus Christ. It's the hand of God. When the Lord pours out His grace upon a nation, He does it at all levels, and you see it reflected in the army, the justice system, the prison fellowship, as well as in the people all across the country.

Rwanda as a nation sought God because it was desperate, and God answered because He is a loving God. That is what is behind our healing and the power of our reconciliation, and it is available to the entire world. The God who is healing and blessing Rwanda wants to heal and bless the entire world if it will but call upon Him.

Notes

Two: Setting the Time Bomb

1. Gerard Prunier, *The Rwanda Crisis: History of a Genocide* (New York, Columbia University Press, 1995), 26–27.

2. Ibid., 52.

3. Ibid., 50.

4. Adam Hochschild, *King Leopold's Ghost* (New York: Houghton Mifflin, 1998), front matter.

Four: The Countdown

1. Antoine Mupenzi (Kinigi villager who fled Rwanda), in discussion with the author, August of 2005.

2. Kayitsinga Fautsin (Rwandan Tutsi), in discussion with the author, July of 2005.

Five: A Carefully Laid Plan

1. International panel of eminent personalities, "Rwanda: The Preventable Genocide", (www.visiontv.ca/RememberRwanda/ReportWordDoc.doc).

2. Linda Melvern, *Conspiracy to Murder: The Rwandan Genocide* (New York: Verso, 2004), 225.

3. Anonymous (a man imprisoned for war crimes during the genocide), in discussion with the author, August of 2005.

4. Ibid.

5. Roméo Dallaire, *Shake Hands with the Devil: The Failure of Humanity in Rwanda* (New York: Carroll & Graf, 2004), 146–47.

6. Ibid., 150.

7. Ibid., 224.

8. Ibid., 226.

9. Ibid., 245.

10. Ibid., 255.

11. Ibid., 268.

12. Ibid., 160.

13. Ibid., 278–80.

14. Prunier, *The Rwanda Crisis*, 254.

16. Philippe Gaillard, interview by *Frontline*, PBS, September 12, 2003 (www.pbs.org/wgbh/pages/frontline/shows/ghosts/interviews/guillard.html).

17. Dallaire, *Shake Hands*, 286.

18. Ibid., 335.

19. Ibid., 272.

Six: The Demons Unleashed

1. Javan Sebasore, in discussion with the author, August of 2005.

2. Ibid.

3. Ibid.

4. Ibid.

5. Ibid.

6. Ibid.

7. Ibid.

8. Ibid.

9. Ibid.

10. Valentina Iribagiza, interview by *Frontline*, PBS, for "Ghosts of Rwanda" (documentary), March 31, 2004 (www.pbs.org/wgbh/pages/frontline/shows/ghosts/etc/script.html).

11. Anonymous (a man imprisoned for war crimes during the genocide), in discussion with the author, August of 2005.

12. Anonymous (woman from Ruhengiri province), in discussion with the author, August of 2005.

13. Antoine Mupenzi (Kinigi villager who fled Rwanda), in discussion with the author, August of 2005.

14. Anonymous (woman from Ruhengiri province), in discussion with the author, August of 2005.

15. Ibid.

16. Ibid.

17. Ibid.

18. Anonymous prisoner, in discussion with the author in August of 2005.

19. Prunier, *The Rwanda Crisis*, 247.

20. Anonymous (a man imprisoned for war crimes during the genocide), in discussion with the author, August of 2005.

21. Gitera Rwamuhizi (a Hutu farmer), interview by Frontline, "Ghosts of Rwanda."

22. Shaharyar M. Khan, *The Shallow Graves of Rwanda* (London: I. B. Tauris & Co., Ltd, 2001), 15–16.

23. Anonymous (a man imprisoned for war crimes during the genocide), in discussion with the author, August of 2005.

24. Dallaire, interview by Frontline, PBS, 2003, www.pbs.org/wgbh/pages/frontline/shows/ghosts/interviews/dallaire.html.

25. "Vatican Response to Rwandan Nuns' Conviction," *Catholic World News*, June 11, 2001, www.cwnews.com/news/viewstory.cfm?recnum=15710.

26. Frs. Augustin Ntagara, Callixte Kalisa, Aloys Nzaramba, Jean Baptiste Hategeka, and Fabien Rwakareke, in a letter to bishops of the Catholic Church in Rwanda, quoted in Ndahiro Tom, "Genocide and the Role of the Church in Rwanda," *News from Africa* (online), April 16, 2005 (www.newsfromafrica.org/newsfromafrica/articles/art_10231.html).

27. Ibid.

28. Gahiga Nsengiyumva, quoted from text at the memorial at Kigali.

29. Carl Wilkens, interview by *Frontline*, PBS, November 19, 2003, www.pbs.org/wgbh/pages/frontline/shows/ghosts/interviews/wilkens.html.

30. Ibid.

31. Dallaire, *Shake Hands*, 369–70.

32. Gregory "Gromo" Alex, interview by *Frontline*, PBS, October 18, 2003, www.pbs.org/wgbh/pages/frontline/shows/ghosts/interviews/gromo.html.

33. Former President Bill Clinton, statement issued on April 7, 1994, quoted in *100 Days of Slaughter*, www.pbs.org/wgbh/pages/frontline/shows/evil/etc/slaughter.html.

34. Gaillard, interview by *Frontline*.

35. Dallaire, *Shake Hands*, 90.

36. Ibid., 339.

37. Convention on the Prevention and Punishment of the Crime of Genocide (online) (adopted by Resolution 260 (III) A of the United Nations General Assembly on 9 December 1948), www.hrweb.org/legal/genocide.html.

38. Christina Shelley (State Department spokeswoman), April 28, 1994, quoted in *100 Days of Slaughter*.

39. Mike McCurry (State Department spokesman), at a press briefing, May 25, 1994, quoted in *100 Days of Slaughter*.

40. Shelley, at a State Department briefing, June 10, 1994, quoted in *100 Days of Slaughter*.

41. Ibid.

42. Ibid (NOTE : this quote appears in the video *100 Days of Slaughter*)

43. Ibid

44. Ibid.

45. Dallaire, *Shake Hands*, 375–76.

46. Ibid., 89–90.

Seven: Bodies in the River

1. Prunier, *The Rwanda Crisis*, 292.

2. Office of the Press Secretary, "Statement by Press Secretary on Rwanda," July 15, 1994, www.clintonfoundation.org/legacy/071594-statement-by-press-secretary-on-rwanda.htm.

3. Ibid.

4. Dallaire, *Shake Hands*, 472.

5. Ibid., 429–30.

6. Ibid., 431.

7. Prunier, *The Rwanda Crisis*, 299.

Eight: Machetes into Plowshares

1. Prunier, *The Rwanda Crisis*, 314.

2. Philip Gourevitch, *We Wish to Inform You That Tomorrow We Will Be Killed with Our Families: Stories from Rwanda* (New York: Picador USA, 1998), 287.

3. Ibid., 221.

4. Ibid., 296.

5. UN press conference, November 8, 1996.

6. Gourevitch, *We Wish to Inform You*, 308.

7. Ibid.

8. Dallaire, *Shake Hands*, 466–67.

9. Gourevitch, *We Wish to Inform You*, 233.

10. Ibid., 237.

11. Ibid., 303.

12. Ibid., 304–5.

13. Ibid., 305.

14. Ibid., 307.

15. Ibid., 308.

16. Ibid.

17. Ibid., 312–13.

18. Ibid., 308–9.

19. Ibid., 310.

Nine: Uncovering the Truth

1. Gourevitch, *We Wish to Inform You*, 337.

2. Associated Press, "100 Convicted in Rwanda Genocide Trial," August 4, 2003, available online at: www.ctv.ca/servlet/ArticleNews/story/CTVNews/20030804/rwanda_genocide_030804?s_name=&no_ads=.

3. Gourevitch, *We Wish to Inform You*, 318.

Ten: Changing Hearts

1. Deo Gashagaza, in discussion with the author, August of 2005. NOTE: Other than several quotes from Deo, the rest are from the Bishop quoting himself.

Eleven: Forgiveness

1. Houston News Service, "Albright Says U.S. Mishandled Rwanda Crisis in '94," November 9, 1997, www.chron.com/content/chronicle/world/97/12/10/albright.2-0.html.

2. Ibid.

3. Former President Bill Clinton, "Speech by President to Survivors Rwanda," March 25, 1998, www.clintonfoundation.org/legacy/032598-speech-by-president-to-survivors-rwanda.htm.

4. Ibid.

5. Ibid.

6. Kofi Annan (UN Secretary-General), in an address to the parliament of Rwanda, May 7, 1998, available at www.un.org/News/Press/docs/1998/19980506.SGSM6552.html.

7. Dallaire, *Shake Hands*, 322–23.

8. Gregory H. Stanton (President, Genocide Watch), "The Eight Stages of Genocide," www.genocidewatch.org/eightstages.htm.

About the Authors

Anglican Bishop John Rucyahana (b. 1945; a Tutsi) was elected Bishop of the Shyira diocese of Rwanda in 1997. During his term, John often escaped death, even as many pastors, friends, and family members were killed in the ongoing genocide. John works tirelessly for a spiritual renewal in Rwanda; having founded the Sonrise orphanage for children orphaned in the genocide, and ministering in prisons to its perpetrators. He and his wife, Harriet, have five children.

James Riordan is the author of twenty-five books including the *New York Times* bestseller *Break on Through: The Life and Death of Jim Morrison*. His writing has won four Tellys, eight Crystal Communicators, and has been nominated for an Emmy. He also works with troubled teens through Make It Stick and is very involved in prison ministry.

THE CAMPAIGN TO MAKE
POVERTY HISTORY
WWW.ONE.ORG

There is a plague of biblical proportions taking place in Africa right now, but we can beat this crisis, if we each do our part. The first step is signing the ONE Declaration to join the ONE Campaign.

The ONE Campaign is a new effort to rally Americans—ONE by ONE—to fight the emergency of global AIDS and extreme poverty. We are engaging Americans everywhere we gather—in churches and synagogues, on the internet and college campuses, at community meetings and concerts.

Together, we can make a difference in the lives of the poorest of God's children. We invite you to join the ONE Campaign.

To learn more about ONE, please visit **WWW.ONE.ORG**

This campaign is brought to you by